Barbara Yelin

IRMINA

Published in English in 2016
by SelfMadeHero
139 –141 Pancras Road
London NW1 1UN
www.selfmadehero.com

Historical consultancy: Dr Alexander Korb

Original German edition:
Editorial assistant: Christian Maiwald
Editor: Michael Groenewald
Corrections: Gustav Mechlenburg

English edition:
Translated from German by Michael Waaler
Publishing Director: Emma Hayley
Sales & Marketing Manager: Sam Humphrey
Publishing Assistant: Guillaume Rater
UK Publicist: Paul Smith
US Publicist: Maya Bradford
Designer: Txabi Jones
With thanks to: Dan Lockwood

A CIP record for this book is available from the British Library.

ISBN: 978-1-910593-10-3

10 9 8 7 6 5 4 3 2 1

Printed and bound in China.

Barbara Yelin

IRMINA

Afterword by Dr Alexander Korb

Some years ago, I found a box of diaries and letters among my late grandmother's things.

That find was the inspiration behind this graphic novel.

But what I really discovered in that box was a question – a disturbing question about how a woman could change so radically. Why did she turn into a person who did not ask questions, who looked the other way, one of the countless passive accomplices of her time?

The historical background to this story has been carefully researched, and advice was provided by the historian Dr Alexander Korb. If you want to learn more about the historical context, I would highly encourage you to read his afterword at the end of this book.

I have, however, used artistic licence for the plot: the people represented here, their biographical relations and many of the settings have been freely interpreted for dramatic purposes. All names are fictitious.

I would particularly like to thank my family for permitting me this freedom and encouraging me to make this book.

Barbara Yelin, Munich 2015

Part One
LONDON

Oh!

Look...
...over there! On the horizon...

...that dark strip! I think that's it! That's England!

I sure hope so, Miss.
After all, we sail here three times a week.
But I still have to send you below deck now.
Oh no!
Can't I stay a while longer?
Sorry, Miss. I've already made an exception.
Only crew are allowed up here.
A young lady like you hasn't any business on deck. Unless you want to marry the Captain, that is.
Or **me**! How about it, Miss?
I'd rather sign myself up for service.
Hahaha! You're off your head!
Bang

Miss Irmina von Behdinger?

My apologies that you had to wait. It's a real pea-souper outside. You can barely see your hand before your face.
Er... pardon?
Could you... speak a little slower, please? My English...
Don't worry, you'll learn. Come on, the taxi's waiting.

I'm running late. I'll drop you off with my wife.
This exchange... Our Olivia's supposed to learn German, but does it have to be in Stuttgart?
Come along now.

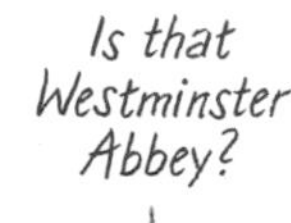

Is that Westminster Abbey?
Could be. Everything looks the same in this fog.

London, 1934.
Station

LONDON
Chronicle
MEADOW

A brandy cocktail, gentlemen?
Thank you.
Enchanting party, Mrs Steale.
Over here!
So thirsty, Henry?
Throat's as dry as the Gobi desert, Jane.
Ah, young Lydia Smith. And your friend from Germany?
Mrs Steale! Yes, this is Irmina.
Irmina von Behdinger.
It is my pleasure, ma'am. Thank you for the invitation!
New faces are always welcome. But please don't stay sitting too long. You must dance!

Oh, she's SO elegant!
I think her earrings are a little ordinary.
Irmina! You simply **always** have to find something bad in everything. Have a drink.
Cocktails? They are only good for a headache.
Good gracious. And with that sourpuss, you'll never be asked to dance.
Blahblahblah. **Oh!** I do believe someone's coming over! Be quiet!
I wonder which of us he'll ask?
Pff. Perhaps I don't want to dance.
Don't you dance?
Oh...
Good. Neither do I.
Oh?
Such silly prancing if you ask me.
And you? New here?
I came with Lydia Smith.

Do I detect an accent? Are you not from here?
Wait... My bet is Sweden. Denmark?
No. Germany.

Germany. Well I never. Emigrated? You don't look remotely Jewish. Don't tell me you're a Communist?
NO!

Oh.
Then what ARE you doing here? Hooking yourself an Englishman, I bet.
What? I...

Come on. You can tell me.
What... no!
I don't want an Englishman! I want a profession, to earn money!

I see. How charming. And how is it going?
Well, I'm just starting out.

But I have been accepted to a commercial school for young women.
I am the only German in the class.

You don't say?! Commercial school? Gracious...
You wish to be independent...
...as a typist?!
Hahaha!
Henry! Control yourself.
And no more brandy. Miss... What was your name again? Irma?
I'm just having a little chat with the girl, Jane. She looked so lonely.
Pff. I don't need to chat with a snob like you.
Well I never! That's enough.
Fetch yourself a drink, Irma. And dance, why don't you?
Amuse yourself!

tap
tap
I can recommend the whisky.
Would you care for one?
-Oh!
Erm, yes please.
I advise against mixed drinks. They only cause headaches.
However, Scottish whisky is like gold in your throat. You really must try it.
And you look like you could do with one.

You think so?
Try it.
Smells of smoke.
Too strong?
Not at all.
IRMINA!
There you are! Oh dear, no one asked you to dance yet?
Lydia! Please!
A good friend?
Lydia sometimes takes me with her so that I can get to know London.

And? How do you like it?

London? Oh, I think it's WONDERFUL! The shops, the hubbub, the theatres, cinemas, the Thames and even the fog! I could drift around for days being amazed!

It's just the Londoners...

I've already been here half a year, but every day they still remind me that I'm not one of them.

You can't imagine how one is treated as a stranger here.

Sure I can. A little.

Oh, forgive me. How stupid of me.
Where do you come from?
You wouldn't know it.
From a tiny island in the Caribbean. A British colony.

The West Indies?
That's right!
Wait.
The Bahamas, Jamaica, Trinidad and Tobago...?

Almost, Miss. But well done anyway. You know more than most of the English.

I've got it. Barbados!
Gosh! That's right!

About 15 degrees latitude and 60 degrees longitude. Agriculture: sugar cane. Capital... Bridgetown?

Well done. Tell me, Miss. Do you know the islands?

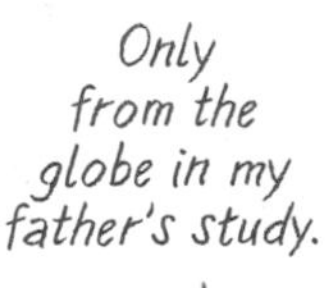
Only from the globe in my father's study.

I used to sit looking at it for hours when he was off travelling.
And he travelled a lot.

I learned all the places with exotic names by heart.
And I wanted to become a captain once I was old enough, and sail the seas.
Discover unknown islands, find treasure, solve the mystery of Atlantis... all those kinds of things.
Ambitious plans, Miss.
Yes, well. So far I haven't made it further than across the Channel.
But I do what I want, you know?

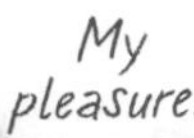

Thank you, lad.
It took longer than expected, but I can take over again.
My pleasure.

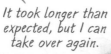

Enjoy your evening, Miss.
Hold on... You're **not** the bartender?
No.

But...
...don't run away so fast!
What are you doing here, then?
You may not believe it, young lady...

...but I'm here as a guest.
Oh! Of course.

Do you know Henry over there?
We're fellow students. I came with him.
Him? I've already had the... pleasure.

You're a **student**?
Indeed. At Oxford.

Oxford?! Really? How did you manage that?
I mean, I've read an awful lot about it. Only the best are accepted and it costs a **mountain** of money!
I have a scholarship from Hertford College.

A scholarship?! Good grief, you must be incredibly wise!
Oh, Oxford. What I would give to walk those hallowed halls just once.
You should come and visit me, Miss.
What? Really? You would...

My goodness, a thimble would be bigger...
...but I wouldn't want to impose...
Sir?
THERE you are, Howard! And look who it is...
...the typist. Oh, so you'll talk to **him**, I see.
Not scared of the bogeyman, hmm?
Henry! You're drunk. Please leave us in peace.
Here's to the beautiful couple!
The German typist...
...and the beggar student.

Hang on!
Now I understand, Miss...
You follow only the orders of your **Führrrerrr**...
Henry!

Gerrmans, choose brrrrown!!

But I think you may have misunderstood the point? **Hahaha!**
Henry!!

That's enough for today!

Oh, he's always so... so naughty.
Please have another drink...

Thank you. I think we will be going.
Thank you for the charming evening.

Irmina?
How un-pleasant.
Miss!

Your coat!

Miss...

How are you able to remain so calm?!
He was drunk. Don't dwell on it.
And the others? They just look on in amusement! Why doesn't anyone say anything?
Miss, as you may be able to imagine...
...I have experienced such scenes more than once before.
The best thing to do is to pay them as little attention as possible.
Oh! You're shivering.
Please take your coat.

Should I accompany you home?
Oh...
I can manage by myself...
Understood. Then I shall take my leave.
Oh.
Good evening.
...
Howard?

Howard!
Would you really show me around Oxford?

...OUR COR - RES - PON - DENCE... ON THE FIF - TEENTH OF MAY...

Klack klack
klack
REG - ARD - ING OUR AG - REE - MENT...
...ON THE NINE - TEENTH OF MAY IN THE YEAR NINE - TEEN THIR - TY - FOUR...

ASS - UR - ANCE OF GRA - TI - TUDE AND THANKS...

Tell me. Did you kiss? Everyone was talking about you after you left!

Lydia, **please**. I must concentrate.

Klack Klack Klack

Klack Klack

Klack Klack

But I'm sure he tried. Am I right?

If I were seen with a man like **that**...

Klack Klack

...I REP - EAT...

...all hell would break loose. You're lucky. Your parents are in Germany.

I heard...

Irmina! I thought we were going to Krickenham's?

No time!

I'm going to see Aunt Hedwig in Norwich. My train leaves soon from Paddington!

Oxford Station, June 1934.

You really came.

Of course. I said I would.

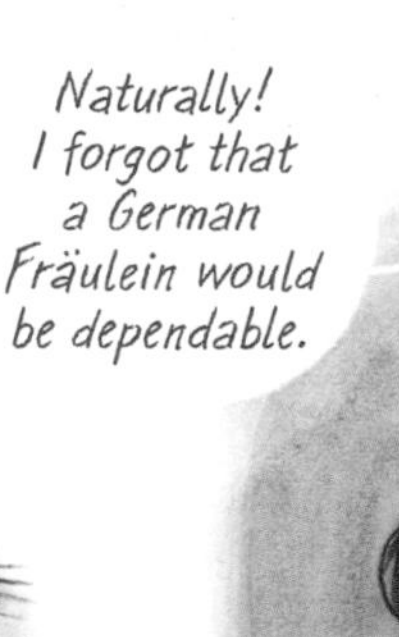

Naturally! I forgot that a German Fräulein would be dependable.

Welcome to Oxford! And now?

Show me your university?

Ok. What shall we see first?
Oh, that I know already: the libraries!

I read in one of my father's books that there are stacks of them here!
Well then, if you'll escort me. It's not far.

Here you can see...
...Carfax Tower. At almost 900 years old, it's Oxford's oldest sentinel!
But there are also others who watch over the people here: the gargoyles.
Who?!

Look up there.
Oh! A bug-eyed monk!

And another one! And there, a dragon! Haha!
Medieval water-spouts.

You must take care not to find yourself beneath one when it rains.

And where is the university?
You're in the middle of it! This is all a university.
Up ahead to the right is Oriel. Left is All Souls, and behind it Hertford College.

And here is the Radcliffe Camera, part of the University library!
Oh! Not rain again! I sometimes wonder how the English can bear such summers.

Or, at least, what they call summer... Come on!
Are we allowed in?

Well, let's try. But be careful...
...the entrance is guarded by another dragon.

Dragon? I don't see one!

Miss!
Yes, you! MISS!! Stop!
Huh?

I don't know you. What are you doing here? Which college do you attend? And your name?
Madam...

Madam... "Reputation is an idle and most false imposition, oft got without merit and lost without deserving."

Howard Green! Oh, if only the English students were half as well read as you...
Miss Bedwin, please grant me a favour...

Psst... all good. We can go in, but we must be quiet.

Psst... what was that old-fashioned English?

Oh...

That was from "Othello".

"Othello"?

Well, Miss Bedwin is feared by every student.

But I please her occasionally with quotes...

Ah, so you tamed the dragon with Shakespeare?

Miss Bedwin was one of the first female students to attend Oxford. Her knowledge of Shakespeare is superior to that of many of the professors.

But it's only recently that women have been permitted to graduate. For her, it came too late.

And how is it **you** know "Othello" by heart?

The language of Shakespeare was the English we learned in school – in contrast to the Bajan dialect of the simple people.

We were taught that everyone spoke so in our venerable motherland.
And so I was forced to make the discovery that no one understood my bookish diction!

So many books...
And this is just a fraction of the total. Here is where English literature and history are preserved.

My speciality is law...

Irmina?

Look. There's Berlin!

And there... Barbados.
If I were to study, it would be geography.

But at the moment they say at home that studying isn't for German women.

It is something only for blue-stockings.

Bluestockings? **Hahaha!**
And you abide by that?

Women who study betray their... purpose. Women serve their country in other ways. You understand?

Good gracious...
But don't tell me that you've come here to spread such nonsense? With all due respect, I won't believe it.

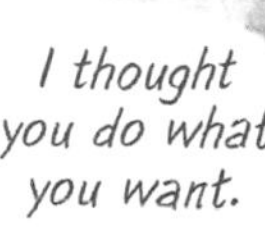
I thought you do what you want.

My two brothers received all the money we had for an education.

There was nothing left.
So I dropped out of school before graduation. What use would it be?

Look. The rain has stopped.

Come with me.
What?

Miss Bedwin! "Welcome ever smiles, and farewell goes out sighing."
Adieu, Miss Bedwin.

Look, there is the venerable Hertford College...

...and this is the world-famous Bridge of Sighs!
But we have other plans.
Wait here!

...
I'll be right back.

Hahaha!

DRRING DRRING

Hop on!
But...

...where are we going?
You'll have to wait and see.

Hold tight!
We're there. Ready to board, Captain?

But... we can't just take a boat, can we?
Of course.
Jump in.
I'm a member of the Hertford rowing club.
Oh...
A punt?
You'll have to make do with it for today.
This reminds me of Spreewald!
My uncle has a country house there I used to visit in summer.
Occasionally I was allowed to take out a punt..

...and I would let the water take me. I used to think, if I waited long enough, that I would maybe even reach the sea.
And then I would find work aboard an ocean liner and sail to America.
Oh really? In Barbados, there is a beach with huge rocks lying in the swell, as if thrown there by giants.
From there I could sometimes see the ocean liners from Europe passing by as they crossed the Atlantic!
I often sat there. I would have waved to you aboard your ocean liner!
What?! How enviable! And you really would have kept watch for me the whole time?

Hmm, well, no. also had to study ometimes. Actually, lmost all the time, to be honest.
Or I played football with the others, on the way to school, with a breadfruit as a ball - until it split. Or until Godma caught us.
So, it could well have been that you would have sailed by unnoticed...
Haha! Later I found out that in Spreewald it's only possible to go in circles.
So my hopes of reaching the sea fell through...

Miss...

You really should allow me to take the helm.
What will people think?

Is this a mutiny, sailor?
Not at all! Haha. Aye-aye, Cap'n!

My goodness...

...what I would give to see the Caribbean...

Well, if you keep up this speed...
...we'll be there soon.

Seriously. If you work as you punt, you will achieve much, Irmina.
However, what do you think of taking a short break?
Take in some supplies on land?
You mean sea biscuits?
I fear that supplies are limited here. But perhaps you like apple pie?
Apple pie? I'm persuaded! I love apple pie. Aunt Hedwig makes the best.
I assure you that her pies are worth the trip to Stuttgart.
Stuttgart?

Stuttgart? Irmina, I have nothing against your aunt's pie, but I'd rather not visit Germany at the moment. That Hitler...

Oh, that Hitler! The world has nothing else to say...

...when the conversation turns to Germany.

I can't hear it any more.
Hitler...
...Hitler...

Hitler!

He won't last long. It's a phase! Of that I'm completely...

Careful!
...certain!

Thud

Splash

Goodness. What were you doing?
Oh, the water's cold!
Quick. It's not far.

Wait...
...now!

Quietly!

Tap
Tap
Tap
Tap
Tap

I don't think any-
one heard us.
Pff

Knock Knock
Howard? Open up!
Come on, Howard! I heard something.
Who is it?
Me. Lester. Open up!

What do you want?
I need your essay on civil law.

How about you write an essay yourself for a change?
No time! Why is there a puddle of water out here?
Oh... I have a visitor...
What?!

It's a mermaid.
Don't be cheeky, darkie!
Goodbye, Lester.
Click

Miss?

Cap'n, it's safe to come out from cover now.
Aa-tchoo!!
What am I going to do now?
sniff
Well, first change into some dry clothes.
I hope they fit.
In the meantime, I'll try to rustle up some tea.
I...
Don't worry, Miss. I'll take my time.
Click
Thanks.

Knock Knock
I was only able to bring up one cup without raising suspicion.
It's the rowing club kit.
A little large, I fear.
And I usually don't wear trousers...
It looks wonderful on you. Like Marlene Dietrich in "Morocco"!
Your tea. I'm sorry it took so long.
Oh, I...
...I was looking at your photos.
Is that your fiancée?
She's very pretty.
My mother.
She went to America when I was five.
And she left you behind?
My father had just died and she had to work.
My brother and I were raised by my godmother.

And my other siblings went to live with Uncle Thomas. But you're still freezing. Wait a moment...
...I still have this...
Whisky? Again?
For emergencies and special occasions.
Oh? And which is it today?
Well, I'm not often visited by a mermaid.
Haha! I'm certainly getting used to it.
By the way, where's your roommate?
Who? No. I live alone.
But the second bed?
There was an odd number of students as the rooms were assigned.
This room - well, the other gentlemen prefer their own company.
You understand.
Oh...

How fortunate you are to have a... single room.
Please, have a sip.
I'm warm enough.

Well, you haven't left much, Cap'n.
Then you'll have to drink whisky without tea.

As you wish. But just a drop.
Come on! Down with it!
In one GO!

GO!!
cough

The train!! The evening train to London!
My train!

When does it leave?
It doesn't! It's just gone! The next one isn't until morning!
Oh, heavens above! How could I have been so careless!!
But it's MY fault.
What now?
Howard...
...do you think it's perhaps possible...
In London, they think I'm visiting Aunt Hedwig.
Could I not simply...

...be your room-mate until morning?

NIGHT OF
THE LON
KNIVES
These **Germans!**
They've gone totally mad.
Morning Pos
100 ARE KILLED IN GERMAN RE
NIGHT OF THE LONG KNIVES
Creak
Good morning.
You're late to breakfast.
I'm sorry.
And what do you look like?
I... overslept.
Irmina, as long as you're living here, you live by our rules. We breakfast at eight o'clock on the dot!
What time did you even get home last night?

I... it must have been shortly after nine. I was visiting Aunt Hedwig...

Ow!

Oh yes...? You don't want your bacon, do you, Irmina?

N... no. **Please** take it.

It's unbelievable! They report at least a hundred dead.

I wonder, Marjorie...

...whether we should bring Olivia home.

What?!

Will that mean Irmina has to go back to Germany?

Quiet, Gertie.

But Irmina, what are your Germans **doing** over there?!
This is insanity!

Erm... what? How so?
What on earth has happened?

Hitler has had the SA Chief of Staff, Röhm, arrested and his people killed. Shot openly on the streets!

What? But...
...but why?! And... what can I do about it?
As if how they treat the Jews and Communists wasn't bad enough...
Now the Nazis are killing their own people!
The Germans are ANIMALS!
Terrible.

Irrrmina!!!
Arrre you always decent?
Anyway, nothing ever happens in Stuttgart! And besides...
Irrrrmina!
Heehee
Haha
...they are not MY Germans.
Why don't you English mind your own affairs?!
IRMINA, that's QUITE enough!
NO!!!
Morning!
They've found the LEGS!
Morning!

"Gruesome find. Two amputated legs found in a suitcase in a locker in King's Cross Station. It seems likely that the legs belong to the head found in Brighton."

The Brighton Trunk Murderer?!

They still haven't caught him?

That **monster**. I told you that it wasn't over!

Terrible.

"'I GAVE THE **OR - DER** TO BURN OUT THE **TU - MOURS**. HE WHO LIFTS HIS HAND FOR A **BLOW** MUST **KNOW** THAT **DEATH** IS HIS **FATE**.' WITH THESE WORDS..."

"...HERR **HIT-LER** LAST NIGHT SOUGHT TO JUS - TIFY THE RE - CENT EXE-CU - TIONS IN **GER - MANY** TO THE REICHS - TAG."

Dictation over! Leave your typed sheets on my podium!
Now, your marks from last week!

Psst, Lydia!
Are we still going to Krickenham's for lemonade?
Miss Jane: pass!

Miss Gwendolyn: fail! Learn to concentrate!
I have to tell you something...

Miss Kitty: just about passed!
Miss Irmina: not a single mistake. The only one of you!
Discipline, obedience, hard work! **German** virtues! Let her be an example to all of you!
Miss Lydia: pass!
Whisper
Whisper
Whisper
That **Nazi** Fräulein!
So, are you coming?
I...
...I've already got plans, Irmina.
Your lemon-ade.

August 1934.
Evening paper! Hindenburg dead! **Hitler Reich President!**

Really?
We're allowed to walk on the grass?
Have you never been here?
My host parents don't want me going to Hyde Park alone.
How fortunate that you have Aunt Hedwig with you today.
Haha! Precisely! It's wonderful here. And it's so big!
Did you know that the park measures almost three miles across?
Oh yes?
Well, Aunty! Let's see...
...how far you manage!
Hey! Wait!

Phew...
Besides, my host parents have nothing to say to me anyway.
Oh?
Their daughter is returning from Germany early.
So, there's no room for me any more, they say.
But Irmina, what are you going to do?!
I don't know yet. The money my parents give me isn't enough to rent a room.
The school fees take up most of it...
Wait! Perhaps I have an idea. I made the acquaintance of an old lady at the rowing club's annual party.
Come on, walk with me and I'll tell you about her.

I'm going to graduate soon anyway...
Then I'd be in-dependent!
...and earn my own money! I'll finally be...
...free...
Howard?
Where are you going?
Look. Something's going on over there...
Is that Speakers' Corner?
For Heaven's sake, get out of here!!
Haven't you eyes in your head? That's a gang of blackshirt fascists!!

This way, please.

Knock Knock
The German girl is here, Countess.

Oh, there you are.
Come in.

Good day, Countess.
Has Brenda shown you the room?
I believe everything has been prepared satisfactorily.

Cough
From Germany, are you?
Very young, aren't you?

Nineteen, Countess.
A child!
And you have emigrated here? Jewish?

N... no -
neither.
I...
I'm simply
a normal
German.
A NORMAL
German?
Child,
you don't
understand
what you're
saying!
And it appears that
it is just the beginning.
Don't you read the
newspapers?
You
normal
Germans are
wreaking
havoc.
Oh, news-
papers...
Child!
You have
much to
learn.
Is that
YOU?!
...Yes.
Over thirty
years ago.
For
wearing
trousers...

...they
almost threw
us in prison.

So, you
really were a
suffragette?
Indeed.

I was. It's us
you have to thank
for your vote,
young lady.
I'm not
allowed
to vote
yet.

Only at
twenty-
one.
Then you'd
better hurry!
German women
have already
had their passive
voting rights
withdrawn.

And from
the look
of it, you'll
have no vote
at all soon.

So, what are
we to do with
you? You have
no money?

Money
I don't need. But I do
need a companion.
You will
accompany
me to public
occasions.
Usually,
I only take on
immigrants.

Sigh
You are still much too young to know if you wish to belong to the immigrants...
...or your so-called normal Germans.

Oh well. We'll give it a go. You may stay.
The young Oxford student with the impeccable manners...

...put in a very good word for you.

Tomorrow you will accompany me to a Labour Party social committee.
Thank you, Countess.

I'm tired.
Good-night.

..and just ima-gine it, I have my own fire-place!

Dear Mother and Father,

From today, I am living in the home of an old
ountess. My room is spacious and even has its ow
throom. Not only that, but I also receive wonderfu
meals each day. She takes me everywhere with her,
ch as to talks and social engagements. I meet many
people in the Labour Party and I am discovering
London again from a completely different point
f view. She fights each day against poverty and

DAILY WORKER

Working Women! Fight Against War

WOMEN

ANTI-FASCIST ACTIVITIES

British Museum, November 1934.

She is incredibly influential and affluent!

She doesn't have to do anything the whole day long...

...and yet she never stops trying to make the world a better place and to help the poor.

And she wants me with her everywhere she goes.

I'm constantly out and about with her...
...as well as at commercial school every morning.
So you see...
...even if you visited me more often...
...I wouldn't have any time.
Irmina.
My exams are around the corner.
Studying law is not child's play.
That's why I visit London so rarely at the moment.
I'm studying day and night. You know that...
...passing my exams is my highest priority.

I don't know. What use is it to be so educated?
In the end, we're all alone like the old Countess.
But you also want to earn money! Have a pro-fession!
Yes, I do.
But I want **MORE** than just to learn!
Maybe... I should just go back to Germany.
What?! What are you talking about? You have your exams soon!
Precisely! But it's always **YOUR** education that's more important!
Irmina! What's gotten into you today?!
Don't be so **foolish**!
Oh! So now I'm foolish?!
And you? You're always the cleverer one?!
It's easy for **you**! You've got your scholarship!
Easy?!
Irmina, you have **no** idea how hard I had to work...
...to get that!

In Germany, someone like **you** wouldn't get anything at all!
What?!

Howard?
Howard! I'm sorry.
Shhh!
You're right. I am foolish.
I'm sorry.

I'm sorry. I was talking nonsense.
You are aware of what's going on in Germany right now, aren't you?
I can't do anything about that! It's nothing to do with me!
Oh, Irmina. Sometimes I really wonder who you are.
Me? But... you know already.
Typist!
Bluestocking!
Communist!
Nazi Fräulein!
Emigrant!
Suffragette!
I'm me. Isn't that enough?
I just want...
Can't we see each other more often?
Cough

Just look at all those people down there.
They buy elegant clothing, eat wonderful foods, do what they want. I'd like to be able to do and forgo what I want, too. Wouldn't you?
Maybe. But first we have to pass our exams.
Who knows what awaits us after that.

Sussex, December 1934.

Ah, Jeremy...
I hope you have prepared everything as discussed.

A bicycle?

But I can't ride a bicycle!
Well then, you will learn.

Like so, Miss...

...and now pedal!
Ouch!

Oh dear! What do I do? Ah!
Pedal!

It's working!
You can let go, Jeremy!

I'm cycliiing!
Merry Christmas, Irmina.

London, March 1935.
Good afternoon, Countess.
Irmina. How was school?
Oh, the same as always.
Unlike this topsy-turvy world. Before I forget...
...there is a letter for you on the side table.
Thank you.
I have to leave again in a minute, Countess.
REELS at ONRUSH of WAR
CONSCRIPTION IN GERMANY
What?
But...
But what do I do now?
Chime Chime
Goodness. I have to go.
...we are no longer able to send you money each month. The political landscape has resulted in restrictions on foreign exchange trading. It's no longer possible to send money abroad for the foreseeable future. We're sure you will find some other way...

Theater
THE KEY
MAN OF ARAN
The Key
PICTURE HOUS
Howard!
ring ring

I'm sorry I'm late.
I was beginning to think you weren't coming.
I have to tell you something...

Can it wait until after the film?

I queued for tickets for almost an hour.

And the screening is about to begin.

You'll like it. It's about the sea.

Good evening, sir.

Ok, it can wait.

What a crowd!

Do you have a ticket?

Of course. Here you go.

I worked like crazy to be able to see you today.

There is a seat there.
Up front in the middle, sir.

There? Hang on a minute... next to the **boy**?
Surely there's another seat?

Sir, the theatre is full. All that's left is at the end.
Well, **he** can sit at the end then.

But I'm not sitting next to someone like him. I've paid good money.
No.

But sir...
I thought this theatre was for Englishmen, not for darkies. I'm not sitting there!
You!

Sir...
Who do you think you are?
Irmina.

Who do you think you're talking about?
Irmina!

You might not believe it, but this man is a citizen of the British Empire...
...with a scholarship to Oxford! Ha! And **you**?!
Stop it!
You're a **prole**! A repulsive, uneducated Englishman!

What's she going on about?!
I'm guessing she's his bit, is she?
You should be ashamed of yourself, girl!
We're going.

You disgusting, worthless...
WE'RE GOING!!

So, now you have a couple more seats free.

PICTURE HOUSE

Beep Beep

Irmina...

Irmina!

Stop!
What?!

...

Why did you do that?
I don't know.

You provoked him.
What?

You're brave...
What?!
But we have to be sensible, Irmina.

Nothing like that can happen again, Irmina! If the university found out...
I **cannot** have any problems. My exams are around the corner.
But what should we...

Just being seen together can cause problems.
For you, too! Don't you see that?
But...
...I did it for you!

No. You did it for YOURSELF.

My education is the most important thing there is right now. NOTHING may be allowed to get in its way.
I'm asking you, please be more discreet.

Oh... nothing. Nothing important.

Klack
Klack
Klack
Klack
Klack
Klack
Klack
Klack
Klack
Miss Behdinger...
Yes?

The bursar had to inform me that you are two months behind on your school fees.
Oh?

Please see that the outstanding amount is settled. We wouldn't want it to affect your graduation.
But...
Of course.

Ok, girls! Break time.
For tomorrow, the text from today twice again.
Clap clap
Your work has also left much to be desired recently.
I must say that you disappoint me.

Irmina, what's wrong?
Aren't you coming to Krickenham's?
No.

I... I still have typing to do.
Klack
Klack
Klack
Klack
whisper
whisper
whisper

Countess...

You are the only person who can help me. I don't see a way out.

No!

Countess, I'm in a desperate situation! The German foreign currency policies...

No!
Again. Matter of fact!

Dear Countess...
...I have some temporary financial problems.

I promise to pay you back!

As soon as I have finished school...
...and I can finally start working.

Then I will earn my own money...

...and will be able to pay you back in full.
Countess!

Countess?
Knock
Knock
And then I will travel the world.

Countess, I...
Oh.

Irmina, it's you! Please come back later. Now is not a good time.

Of course.
Calm yourself, my dear.
No one will harm you here.

Irmina!

Please listen to me...
I have received an immigrant.
She is in a terrible state. You...

You have to understand that she has been through an ordeal.
Irmina, I care deeply for you.
But this troubling situation requires action.

I would like you to find new accommodation.

It should be no problem for you.
You are young and fit.
But this person needs someone to look after her.

I understand.

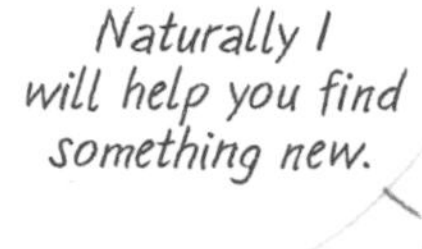
Naturally I will help you find something new.

It's not necessary.

Anyway, I wanted to...
...return to Germany.
Clap

GO BACK?
To Germany? Child! That's **madness**!

Irmina!! Have you really thought this through?!

Portsmouth Harbour, April 1935.
I'll be back...

...as soon
as I can.
Is there
really no other
way? Could you
not take on a
little work?

What do
you suggest?
As a maid? As a
washerwoman? In
a pub? Never.
Could I not lend
you some...?
Or
should I let
someone
keep me?

You don't
even have
enough
yourself!

I have to be able
to mind my own
affairs, Howard.
I'll raise
some money
somehow and
come back. A great-
uncle said I can
help him in his
office in Bremen.
We'll see.

And if they don't let you leave again?
Oh, nonsense! And even if...
I do what I want.
TOOOT

The ship!
And will you write?

I'll write.

Goodbye.

Goodbye.

You're excited, too, huh?
Finally getting back to Germany!

We're sailing into the future!
I tell you, things are happening there. We have to be a part of it!
Those loyal British subjects are nice, but backwards-looking.

Germany, that's where the future lies!

Good grief, you look serious.
I thought you were German, too. But maybe not...

You're a statue.

Part Two
BERLIN

Dear Howard, how are you? Once again, it's been a few months since my last letter.

I left my position in Bremen when they told me that they wouldn't raise my pay...

...and I returned to my parents in Stuttgart. I thought I would never get away from there again.

Ring
Ring
But finally I have some news!

But first things first. I had to stay for a while. Mother's nerves made her ill...

...and she was bedridden for almost three months.

Only once she was back on her feet could I begin looking for work again. And just imagine it...

I'm in Berlin!

Mornin'.
Morning, Herbert.
I'm living in curious accommodations...

Good morning to you!
Mornin'.
Morning, Franz!
...with a colourful collection of people...

Irmina. Good grief, you're getting thinner by the day. You have to eat more!
I'll bring you back another rissole this evening.
Thanks, Franz.
Yes! A great German miracle has occurred in these past four years...
...all here for widely different reasons.

Shut up! Goebbels is talking!
Do we have to listen to that stuff in the mornings now, too?
Bye, everyone.
I have to go...
...which in these four years in the exceptional hands of our Führer...
Here in the capital, it's much plainer to see...

...just how much Germany has changed.

But I'm getting used to it.

I'm finally earning my own money (but only a little). Even better, I'm coming back soon, Howard!

I've received help...

...from an influential uncle.

Irmina! Hello!
Gerda!

Plums!
Want some? They're fresh from the tree.
Heaven sent you! I haven't had breakfast.
Since when do you have fruit trees?

An uncle with connections high up!

The old Jewess on the ground floor...
She disappeared suddenly in spring. Probably ran away. I said to mother...
...someone should take the delicious fruit.
Emigrants. Do you know that the English prefer them to normal Germans?

We're late.
Really? Hurry! Last week the old guy totally blew a fuse again.

And I was only a few minutes late.
Recently I was missing a button. That REALLY caused a storm.
JUNO
And he was able to get me a position...
Irmina, he ALWAYS finds some reason...

...to fiddle with your blouse.

* Reich Ministry of War.

I'm supposed to settle into the position for a couple of weeks.

Fräulein von Behdinger, the new manuscripts.
Thanks.

My English skills in particular...

Can I take the others?
Have you already translated them?
...have proved quite useful.

Of course.
And I have been assured that then...

Klack
Klack
Klack
Klack
Klack
Klack
Klack
Klack
...I would be transferred to the German consulate in London!

Heil Hitler, ladies!
Heil Hitler, sir!
I'm expecting news of my transfer any day now.

Hmm, the young lady with the von in her name.
You're a hard worker?
But of course, sir.

Good, good.

We will not let you go so easily.

Jmmer gepflegt und ständig adrett: Du und die Maschine so ist das nett!
But sir, you were going to...
My transfer to London?

Yes, yes, I haven't forgotten.
I'm doing my best for you, Fräulein.
However, do not tax my patience.
This way, sir.

It cant be too long now...

...until I'm back in London.

I will probably have to be patient a little while longer...

...but then I will be crossing the Channel once again! So, see you soon, Howard! And dont forget to write!

Here. Ten marks' rent.
And really? No letter has come for me?

Well, the new girl certainly doesn't natter much.
She's just a little shy.

Fräulein, the administration still needs your documents for the position. See to it.
Very well.

Are you coming to the cinema on Saturday?
"Victoria in Dover".

Oh! I love romantic films!

Juden uner-wünscht
Delicatessen

Patience, Behdinger. Good things take time.

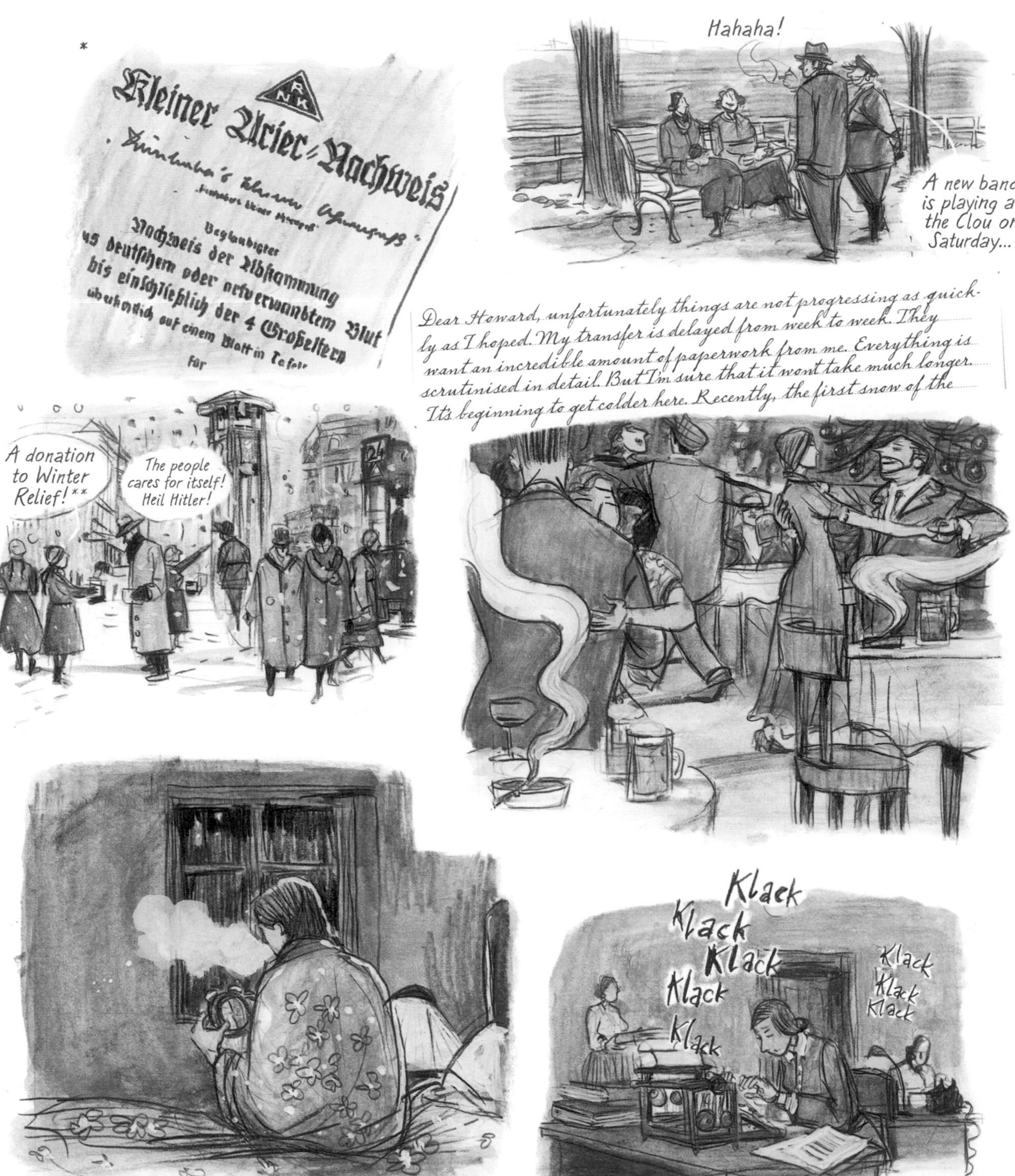

* Aryan certificate: certified proof of ancestry from German or related blood up to and including four grandparents. Obligatory for all official employees.

** Winter Relief: a Nazi propaganda institution which collected money for the poor. Both collecting and giving were obligatory despite being referred to as "voluntary".

January 1937.

Everybody! This is Irmina...
...my cousin, once believed lost to the English!
Haha...

You know Kurt from the Ministry.
Good evening.
And this is Emil, also a lieutenant.
All in civilian clothing. I insisted.
Back there are Fritz and Wilhelm from Hans' office.
Maria and Greta, their better halves...
...and Privy Councillor Mager.
Emma, the drinks!
So, tell me everything, cousin.
It's been absolutely ages!
A liqueur? Moselle?
Oh... do you have whisky?
Hahaha! Irmina! You always were special.
We don't have English drinks here. How about kirsch brandy?
It's actually for the men.
Thank you. I'll have the kirsch.
Here. My goodness, have I heard some stories about you. Did you really elope to England?
RRRinng
What? No! I...

Oh, another guest! Please excuse me.
I'll be right back.

Gregor! You CAME after all!

Gregor Meinrich. Good evening.

I'm sorry, Gregor. Dinner has already been cleared...

No trouble at all, Anne-Marie. With a glass and a sofa...
...you will make me a happy man. I came straight from the office.

May I?

Moselle?
Thanks.

Well, Meinrich?
Work is good, so one hears.

Congratulations, Meinrich. I read in the evening papers...
Well, one may be optimistic, Herr Councillor. We're working flat out.

...that Albert Speer was yesterday named by the Führer as the General Building Inspector for the Reich capital.

A decision of vision. Now he will be able to implement the grand plans for Berlin...
...without the tiresome bureaucracy of those without vision. Speer studied under Tessenow, as I did. I have already received a few contracts through him. A good man.
Do you have a light?

Thank you. I tell you, in Speer's hands, the city planning of Berlin is on the brink of great change.
Mark my words..
...in ten years, nothing will look the same here. Nothing!

Look at this sofa.
Ornate plunder of the last century! Be gone with it!
Gregor! That's an heirloom!
Anne-Marie! You should know better. Courage to greatness, clarity, severity!
...
YOU are staring at me with great severity.
A new face?
Gregor, may I introduce Irmina von Behdinger, new to Berlin.
And cousin, this is Gregor Meinrich, Hans' partner.
A pleasure...
Irmina the Severe...
She was lost to England for almost two years!
Well, aren't we lucky to have found you again.

Why so serious, Fräulein?
Do you miss the English so terribly?
Hahaha!
Herr Architect...
...if you prefer girls who prattle and jest, you should consider keeping the others company.
On the contrary. I admire earnestness, severity.
However, it is rare to encounter.
I'll leave you two in peace.
As in architecture, greatness arises through severity and clarity. That is the **new way.**
What is your opinion of the new architecture?

...

My father knew Gropius.
He revered him. "Form should follow function."

Gropius?! I will admit that we clung to his ideas at the beginning of our studies.

As if we didn't have our own!
However, an instinctive urge prevents me from tying myself too closely to him. He lacks the vision of grandness. Do you understand?
It also quickly became known that he is a Marxist.
He left Germany long ago.

Didn't you know that? It's soulless architecture, Fräulein. Technical, calculating. Jewish.
We must find our own roots. Bring tradition into the new era.
An architectural culture with national roots! With soul, clarity, greatness!
The new Olympic stadium in Berlin, the Reichsparteitag in Nuremburg...
...those are spaces whose architecture is shaped by the masses!

Do you know Italy? The buildings of classical antiquity, the Colosseum... or Castel Sant'Angelo! THAT is majestic and grand.
So you've been to Rome?

I always wanted to go. Tell me, how is it there?

Oh, wonderful.
Imagine a mild May evening, a breeze blows across Trajan's Forum.
Add a bottle of Chianti.

The purity of the ancient architecture, the warmth of the stones, the softness of the Chianti. I must say...
...one wishes never to leave.
Oh. Chianti? THAT doesn't tarnish the German spirit?

Ha! It seems you are not **so** serious after all, Fräulein.
Let's just say that with regard to the wine we should perhaps advance our alliance with Italy.
This Moselle here...

...is reason enough for it.
But don't you dare tell Anne-Marie I said that.

And what exactly took you to cold England?
I was studying there to be a foreign language secretary.
My goodness. You are capable! A rare quality.
And now? You have returned to Germany to get married?
No. I work at the Ministry of War.
Good God!
Then it's doubly good that we have you here again.
I have to dis-appoint you.
I should already have been there for a while now.
I'll soon be returning to London.
Seriously? Return to the fog?
The fog I'll gladly accept.
And what does London offer you that Berlin cannot?
I... I feel free there! I can do and be as I wish.

THAT's what you want? For it to be up to YOU?
What about the shared responsibility of the people? For Germany? For your country?

My country? Herr Meinrich!
Here, I am unable to afford even my own modest costs! I live in an unheated room and subsist on barley broth!

Your construct of ideas may be glorious, but I cannot buy myself a rissole with them.

But we are talking about a vision for all! A great future awaits all who help work towards it. For that, everyone must make sacrifices!
I treasure your grand future, but I prefer to shape my own.

Well, your honesty suits you. And you are brave, if rather careless. Nevertheless, I consider it as you... letting us down.

Letting you down? Oh no. Believe me...

...most people get by fine without me.

And what if you are mistaken?

Perhaps you would like another drink?
Gregor? We need you at the card table!
Haha! No, I...
You mean there's some of the Moselle left?

Anne-Marie!
I'm in conversation right now...
It's ok. Cousin, I would like to go home.

Please, stay sitting.
But...
Adieu.
Adieu, Herr Architect.
Irmina! And you were talking so wonderfully!

Shouldn't Max drive you at least?
It's ok, Anne-Marie. I'll be just fine.

I'm just fine on my own.

A few days later.

...Mother made Königsberger Klopse.
With capers and purée? Oh, that's one of my favourites, Gerda!
Will you invite me next time?
Gemüse
CIGARREN
offen
Eintopf!

Of course, Irmina. You really are ALWAYS hungry! Haha!
It's no wonder.
Am Sonntag mit dem Führer
For me, every day is stew day.

And now they've deducted a donation for Winter Relief from my meagre wages!

"Voluntary". No one asked ME!
Irmina!

Even YOU have to make sacrifices! The people cares for itself!
Sure, Gerda.
But do you really believe the Führer will be ladling water gruel on Sunday? Hahaha!

BE QUIET! Are you stupid?! If someone hears!

That's subversive talk!! I really should report you to the National Socialist Women's League **right now**!
Ok, ok...
I don't want to hear any more of this, Irmina!!
Well, thank God I won't be here much longer. In two weeks at the most...
...I'll be transferred to London. There I'll receive a decent wage. Then I'll be done with stew.
Leis
Fräulein von Behdinger! The Senior Civil Servant wants you in his office immediately!
Klack Klack Klack
Oh, of course.
And here, the new transcripts.
They must be finished by tomorrow!
Go ahead, put them on my desk.
Behdinger. There you are.
Well, take a seat.

Fräulein, it is my pleasure to inform you of splendid news.

Finally, sir!

I put myself out for you, child!

You can remain here with us! We're offering you a permanent position.

What?
But...

Wonderful, isn't it?
My apologies, sir...

...but there must have been a **mistake**!
I am supposed to be transferred to London!

That will not be happening, child.
You will have heard that England is to have a new king. Much is changing there.

Our naval attaché in the embassy is no longer... Anyway, the details are of no interest to you.

A dangerous democracy rules over there, riddled with Bolsheviks and Jews. It's far too risky for a young lady such as you. But don't worry. I managed to contrive it that you may continue here.

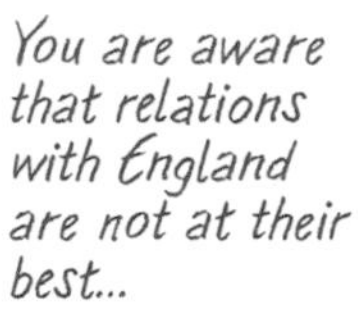

You are aware that relations with England are not at their best...

Oh, look...

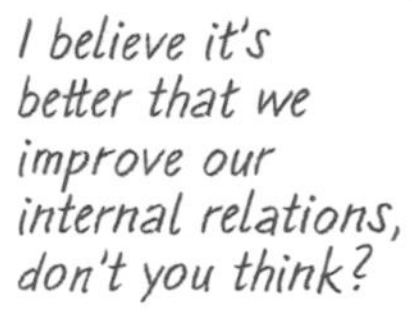

I believe it's better that we improve our internal relations, don't you think?

...you have a loose button on your blouse...

Thank you, sir.

Behdinger.
You can consider yourself lucky that I have made you this offer.
Incidentally, you may also thank your relations.
Now pull yourself together. Heil Hitler.

Was there something else?

Heil Hitler!

Hello?

Fräulein?

Oh, it's **you**!
Where are you going?
We have an appointment.

You're white as a sheet. Are you ok?
I... yes, of course. So, what did you want?
Come on. Let's go somewhere warmer.

A coffee will do you good.
As you wish.

Your coffee, sir.

So, what's so important?
Fräulein, allow me to begin properly...
Firstly, I must apologise in advance.

I do not wish to offend you...
...but for days I have been unable to stop thinking about it...
...and I have an inner compulsion to tell you...
...and I apologise again...
...but I simply have to say it.
I would like to, no, I **must** tell you: it's simply **irresponsible**!
Oh?
But **what**?
Well, that you...
...that you are leaving, Irmina!

What? And why, may I ask?
It's not for a woman such as you.
GERMANY!
Germany needs you now!
There is so much to do here.
Women such as you are needed here.
Don't leave us. Don't go!
Well...
You need not worry for now.
I was told today that I... that I won't be going anywhere for the moment.

Your opinion places you in refined company.
The position in London is no longer vacant for me. I will have to find a new one.
Oh... I see... so you're **not** going?
Well, that's good! Then... I have nothing more to say for the moment.
I beg your pardon? That's **it**?
My apologies.
Fräulein Irmina, perhaps one day we may...
Cough cough
You smoke too much.
I have to return to the Ministry, Herr Meinrich.
Of course. Duty calls. I will not stop you.

CAFÉ UND SPEISELOKAL
Cough
verboten
Juden
Zutritt verboten!

Irmina? You?! So late?

It's a surprise to see you. Don't tell me you're here for the Königsberger Klopse?
N... no, Gerda.
Well, come in. I've just made tea for Mother and me.
Who is it?

Please forgive the disturbance, Frau Guppert.
I'm sure you girls have something to discuss.
I'll give you some peace.
Thank you, Mother.

WHAT?!

You **quit**?!
Yes.

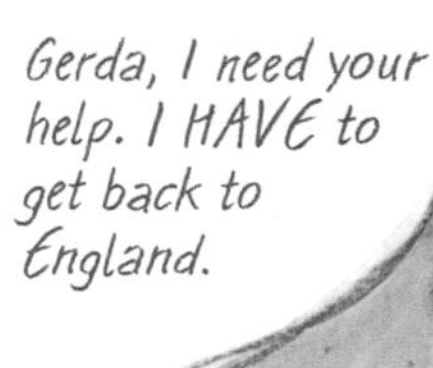

Gerda, I need your help. I HAVE to get back to England.
But WHY, Irmina? Why is England so important?! I don't understand it!!
Please, Gerda, I **can't** tell you. But I don't know who else to ask!
Where can I earn money quickly to pay for the ferry? I have some saved, but not enough.

I don't know... Have you done something wrong? At the Ministry? Irmina, don't get me involved in it!
What have you...

Oh, my goodness.
I've got it!!

It's a **man**, isn't it?
YOU! You enigma! You're in love! With a man in England!

Well, tell me!
Yes.

Wait.

We had far too much jam left over from autumn.

I sold the rest. I can give you forty Reichsmarks.
Mother doesn't know about it.
Edelsorte
Edelsorte

Gerda. I... I can't accept it.
How would I be able to pay you back?

Irmina, is he waiting for you?

I... yes.
I hope.

My goodness, you HAVE to take it! For... love!
Don't wait too long!

Go on, hurry! Buy a ticket!

Thank you, Gerda.

But next time you stay for dinner!
It's ok, Mother.
Goodbye, Frau Guppert!

U
S
ALEXANDERPLATZ

Frau Emmering?
KNOCK KNOCK.
Frau Emmering!
I have to tell you something...

Fräulein von Behdinger! It's late!
It's about the room...
Come back in the morning. I'm off to bed.
Oh, but wait...
...a letter came for you.

From England?!
It **couldn't** have come at a better time! You don't know...
Thank you, thank you!

I'll give you a knock in the morning!

But...

Click

Finally...!

What?!

Gone away
address not known
England
...Address unknown?!

Sind's die Augen, ge
Animator
Pschorr-Haus
Pschorr
EINGAN

Pardon me.

Excuse me. Please let me through.

EDEN
Good evening.

Oh! You **came**!!

I've been trying to reach you for days!
Your landlady always fobbed me off.
I was beginning to worry that you had left after all!

EDEN HOT
Where have you been hiding?
I... I've been indis-posed.
Well, all's well now! You're here! Come on!

My apologies, sir...
...we are booked out tonight.
But I have tickets! See for yourself!
There's nothing I can do, sir. Invitation only.
Please come again next week.
EDEN
But...
Herr Meinrich...
Good evening, sir.
...it was a mistake for me to come anyway. I would like to go...
Hey! Meinrich? Is that you?
Herr Oberscharführer!
Heil Hitler!
Heil Hitler, Meinrich. Your fianceé?
What are you doing standing around out here? Come in, it's cold out!
They're with me.
Very good, sir.

"The ranks tightly closed!" We help our own.
May I?
By God, this evening dress pinches. My Trude forces me to come, but you know what, young lady, I prefer my black uniform.
Well, Meinrich. I hear you're up to great things!
Gruppenführer Ermann returned from the opening of your Thingstätte impressed!
A prodigious rally! A symbol of grandness and pride for the German people!
Yes, German architecture is returning to its roots, Herr Oberschar—
Precisely. We'll give those East Silesian Polish swine hell. Bravo, cheers and Sieg Heil!
Thank you, Herr Oberscharführer. I'm honoured.
To your health. Sieg Heil!
Well, children, now get over there and dance.
You... know each other well?
The Oberscharführer? A comrade from the SS.
You're in the SS?!
Since '33. We're a tight group. But that he invited us to his table...
You must be my lucky charm, Irmina.

Irmina, something has changed about you.

Yes...

You look so beautiful, Irmina.

So very... serious...
You're standing on my foot, Herr Meinrich.

Oh!
My apologies...
It's fine.

It's not so bad.

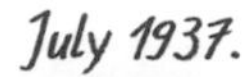
July 1937.

How wonderful that I can show you this today.
It takes my breath away every time I'm here!
My chest is full of might and I feel free in my heart.
Look...

Oh! It really is big. Are there even enough people in the city to fill it?
Well, during the Games last summer, the Maifeld even had to be opened...
...to accommodate all the visitors.

The Olympic Games. Oh, I was still in Stuttgart then.
Irmina, here is where the spirit of our ancestors meets the radicalism of the German restoration.

You designed this?!
No, it's one of March's.
But I'd like to build like this! Do you know...

...ten years ago, while I was studying, Berlin was at a standstill. Nothing was being built.
NOTHING! And then the Führer came. Our boldest dreams could not conceive of such a change!

* Kraft durch Freude (Strength through Joy): a state-run leisure and tourism organisation in Nazi Germany, often used for propaganda purposes.

More flowers...
...and the others are still fresh.

Klack
Klack
Klack
Klack
Klack

November 1938.

...what I've brought you.
Gregor!

Carnations in November? They must have cost a fortune!
I thought you'd like them...

The food is ready.
Wonderful! I have to go out again later. Evening meeting.

What were you writing?
Just my diary, as always.

VÖLKISCHER BEOBACHTER
Paris:
Outrageous! The audacity!
What?
Yesterday's newspaper reports that a Jewish whippersnapper shot the German diplomat Vom Rath in Paris.
Dead?
The Jew? I'm sure he will be soon.
SALZ
No, the other one. The diplomat.
Vom Rath? Critically injured.
Hitler himself immediately dispatched his personal physicians.
That looks wonder-ful.
You have to give the Führer that...

...he takes care of his people.
Why did he shoot?

Revenge! His clan were among those we kicked out during the Polish expulsion.
They haven't been treated with kid gloves. Aren't you eating?

I'm full.

It tastes delicious!

That's enough, Gregor! It **doesn't** taste good!
We both know that I'm a **terrible** cook!

And I don't WANT to cook.

...what's wrong, Irmina?
Ok, ok...

Gregor, cooking should be done by a housemaid!
The household isn't for me. I want to work again.

We've already been through all that. It was you who resigned, after all. And just think about the marriage loan that allowed us to buy all the new furniture.

Well, I've changed my mind. I'm by myself all day just waiting for you.
I've had enough. I'm no good at waiting.

What about your promises of grand achievements? Illustrious society? A spacious apartment? I gave up my name for you.
Irmina! Enough.

Can't we go to Italy again?

I have to be here now.

And we want to have a child. And then you wouldn't be able to work anyway.

But if you joined the party, you could start going to the Women's league.

And crochet with them for Winter Relief? No thanks.

Cough

This rain! Every day it's the same.

Irmina... Actually, I wanted to wait until it was certain. But I just can't keep it from you. I have news.

It's just the step up we need, right?
Well...
He won't get away this time. We've proved our ability and reliability. Speer is already swamped with contracts. They HAVE to include us now!
Goebbels went to Munich with the Führer today. But once he returns...
...I'm sure I'll finally be personally introduced to him.
Oh, Gregor!
Now promise me...
...no more grumbling. Let's stick together now.
Look to the future united.
I promise.

You can rely on me, Gregor.
You know what? I think...
...we'll skip dinner this evening.
Oh yes?
What do you think, my beautiful wife?
Oh, Gregor. Haha!

WRRRRR

WRRRRR

WWRRRRRRRRRR

WRRRRRR
WRRRRRR
Gregor?

smash
smash
WRRRRRRR
JUWELEN
smash
Move it!
WRRRRRRRRRR RRRRRRR

WRRRRRRRRRR

RRRRRRRRRR

RRRRRRRRRR

RRRRRR

Louis!!! But he didn't do anything!

Isn't anyone awake?
Why won't anyone help?!

Gregor...
...are you awake?
Gregor?
...

IRMINA!

Gregor! You scared me.
I couldn't wake you.
I... I couldn't sleep.

You weren't here!

I was needed. I'm just here briefly.
So that you don't worry.
Gregor, last night at the Jew store...

Yes, I just saw.
Irmina, I have to go back. Orders are orders.

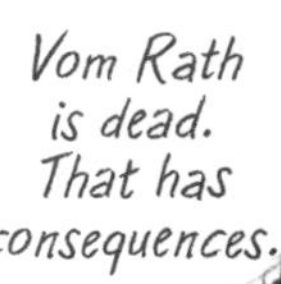
Vom Rath is dead. That has consequences.

Do me the favour...

...of staying home today!
See you later.

Click

Bye.

Empty again.
MILCH
CAFFEE

What's this pigsty here?
Come on, clear the pavement!
SCHMUCKS Inh. Louis

You think you're too good to clean your own mess?!
You don't often see lowlifes working.
No! Not with a broom!
Haha

You use your hands or nothing! Get on with it!

Come on, Erwin, let's go!
Everything's free today!
The Jew shops are all smashed up!
The blighters aren't wrong, eh?
JUDE
Damen-Mode

A little... vulgar, don't you think?
Well, the Jews brought it on themselves.
If they won't listen...
But the produce...
It could still have been used.

Shameful. We should be ashamed.

Irmina?!

Irmina!

Gerda?
What are YOU doing here?

I...
Buying milk.

But I thought you were in London?!

I changed my mind.
smash

As you see. Here I am.

But you so desperately wanted to...
You didn't go?!
Gerda! No!

Cough

And my money? I gave you my life savings!

I know. I still want to return them.
I got married here.

Hey! On the corner of Kantstraße...
You... what?

...that's where the Jew lowlifes live...
Congrat-ulations.

...we gonna give them a polite knock? Hahaha!
Smash

I have to go.

I... just wanted to go shopping.
Crack
I've got to...
I want to go to Frank department store.
Irmina... I don't think it's open today.
Why?
Irmina!
Go to Hertie.
Yes, of course, you're right.

I'll go to Hertie.

Klack
Klack
Klack
Klack
Good evening.
...Good evening.
I have to leave again soon.
What, again?
To the office. I haven't been to the office at all.
Gregor...
...what's going on outside? What... did you... do?
Goebbels stru...
No, the **people's wrath** struck back.
The **people's wrath**?! And you?
And you?
Gre-gor?
WHAT, Irmina?!
You SHOULD NOT go outside.
Not another word.
...
I... and... when are you coming home? I cooked...
As soon as I can.

Klack
Swish

August 1939.

RRRINNG
RRINNG
Hello?
Anne-Marie!

Yes, we finally have a telephone, too...

No, not yet...
Of course, all the preparations...

...have long been in place.

I feel it.

It will all start soon...
Any time now.

KRZZK I will lead this fight KRZZZK
KRZZ also overrrcome KRRZK adverrrsity KRZZZK take the step
KRRZZK ourrr will KRRZ Gerrrman steel
KRRRZKRRRZZ Gerrrmany KRZZZZ
determined never to KRZZ capitulate KRR
KRZZZK

September 1939.
Irmina...
HOSPITAL
WRRUUUUUUUUMM
...a miracle...
...such a little worm!
Halte stets Ordnung
The Obersturmführer sent his congratulations. Even Hans did.
He also had some news, Irmina.
Psst, my son. Germany is growing...
...and it needs us.
A commission in the new territories. Converting a castle - for the Führer himself!
I'm not allowed to say any more, but it will be...
...the contract of our lives.
Gregor!

I know what's on your mind, Irmina. Hans is already there.
Naturally, I will stay here with you two!
Gregor! Called by the Führer. You have to leave immediately! Don't let Hans deny you positions and fame again.
We'll be just fine.
But I...
Sir, visiting hours are over!
clap clap
August 1940.
deutsche Volk seinem Führer echt und Sieg!
Öffentlicher Luftschutzraum
France totally collapses! The front against England!
WARENHAUS KAUF
Juden sind unser Unglück
Stürmer
IKTORIA
Deutschland siegt an allen Fronten

July 1941.
Anyone home?
Reichsfettkarte
EA: Berlin

Goodness, my little worm!
How you've grown again! I've brought you a tin soldier.
Papa!

Gregor...
...you can't call him your little worm forever.
Frieder, hat?
Frieder is almost two.

How are you two?
Oh... we manage. These coal ration cards...
...are already not enough...

It will be a cold winter.
Frieder, leave your father in peace.
But I know it's worth scrimping here, as long as progress is being made.

Little worm, go to your building blocks.
Wah...
Frieder!!
Irmina... we're not getting new materials either.

Anything for the Führer should be of the best materials.
Well, the doors are finished now...
...but the rooms are still missing!

They bring a constant stream of Polack workers.
The barracks are packed with them. Gauleiter has them exercising.
But the building site is at a standstill.

You know that I'm not allowed to tell you this.
But Gregor, it has to start again.

Irmina!!
Aren't you listening?!
It has STOPPED!
Everything goes into **munitions** production now.

Progress isn't being made any more!
But it MUST! It HAS to go on! We're sacrificing so much here!
They even took you out of military service for it!

You don't know what's going on there.
Now goods trains keep rolling through to the East, crammed with Jew—
Gregor!! Not in front of the boy!

We have to persevere. That's what YOU always said.
Otherwise, it's all been for nothing!

There's no fame or honour in building sites any more. They're only found in other fields now.
The Führer has said it plainly. We must show no weakness now.

Gregor! Your brother just died fighting!
Irmina, when the war has been won, people will ask where my medals are.

You're right. No weakness.
Crash

Crash
bam

March 1942.

I'll take it for ten!
Eleven!
Mo-ther...
...what are they doing?
Some people... moved out.
Now their furniture is being auctioned.

Why didn't they take their things with them?

Because they were Jews.

Mother, what are Jews?
Stop asking questions. We have to go to the baker's.

But Mother, what ARE Jews?

Our mis-fortune!
The Jews are our mis-fortune!

Understand?!
Now, be QUIET!
WAAAH!

Hey, little one. Missing your father?
Also at war?
helfen si
sniff
Eastern front.
siegen!
Oh God. Like my son.
It's the worst there.
And we can't do anything.
Deutsche Frauen helfen siegen!
The Völkischer Beobachter reported on more victories only today.
Oh, the newspapers. They're always writing about victories.
My son was just home on leave. He cried and moaned in his sleep. Didn't speak a word during the day. Completely silent. It gave me chills to see.
My goodness...
...how shall our men bravely persevere...
...if you're whining back here? Keep your composure, woman!
Juden unerwünscht
Psst, be careful! They know Goebbels himself!!
sniff

April 1942.

What does father write?
...
Go and play, Frieder!

I'll tell you at dinner.
Stay in calling distance!

...I dont even know when I wrote my last detailed letter. I think it was on the night...

...our unit was holding a section of the curve of the river. In our foxhole...

...and the biting frost. The river was still frozen, so tanks could approach from that direction...

...I took my post around eight o'clock, just as all hell broke loose. The Russians...

...an armed attack with every kind of conceivable heavy weapon. The air whistled and howled, and the explosions...

...I never believed people could withstand what we're going through. The noise and raging...

...terrible to hear how the wounded screamed, lying on the snow in the biting frost where they likely froze...

...as if a hammer had hit me. I collapsed. Between the shoulder blades...

...I'm sending you the grenade shrapnel. Please look after it for me. My dear Irmina, I always promised you...

...be as proud as I am. It is now a man's duty to be out here...

What?
Sniff
...and thanks for the cigarettes.

My knee, Mother! It's bleeding!
Sniff

It's just a graze, Frieder!
Pull yourself together!

Be brave, soldier!
You should be proud.
Your father has been promoted to sergeant.

Click

Klack
Klack
Klack

Mother! Wake up!
Not again!
Have you got your jacket, Frieder?

* Christmas trees: Berlin name for the green marker flares dropped by the Allies before bombing runs.

March 1943.

Frieder, hand me the big hammer...
Ding Dong

Not again...
...we really don't have anything to give.
Irmina, it's me!

Gerda?
What do you want? I paid you back your money long ago.
Irmina, won't you let me in?
What are you doing with that hammer?

Making it darker. Blacking out the windows.
Insufficient blacking out is grounds for punishment, our block leader says.

I know, Irmina. We... I don't have any windows left to black out.
We're bombed out. Almost everything burned.

And... your mother?
Come in. But I don't have anything to offer you.

I wasn't there when the bombs fell. Only Mother was at home.
I don't know where to go...

Ok. Just tonight, Gerda.
Frieder can show you the fold-up bed.
Hello, Frieder.
Hello.
And your husband?
Eastern front.

I still have a little bread. But I really can't give you much.
The relief organisation will look after you now.

I stood there the whole day today. I didn't even get to see someone.
Gerda, you must not despair now, do you hear?
Wait. I still have a jar of preserves.

I was keeping it for a special occasion.
I'm sure it's hard, Gerda...
...but we have to endure! Don't you have anyone else?

Yesterday I thought I could go to the old Clou and stay there. I used to work there.
It was a stupid idea. It's closed, like almost everything since the war began.

It's up here somewhere...
But I didn't even think about it. I just went there.
There were a load of SS men. Vans kept bringing people, who they shoved into the Clou...
What? Oh, **there** it is!
They were Jews. I saw their stars. I wanted to get away quickly...
You have to speak louder, Gerda.
One of them, a boy. He defended himself. The SS men hit him with the butts of their rifles. It – it made a loud crack. Then the boy fell down...
I wondered how I could hear that crack... when I wasn't even very close...
The boy... he just lay there...
I can't get that sound, that crack, out of my head...
My sister-in-law heard from her brother...
...they're taking them all to the East now, where they kill them...
NO!
Smash
What a disaster!
That was the last jar!
I picked them in Grunewald forest...
...with Gregor!

Irmina, it won't be the last attack on Berlin. Take Frieder and go NOW to Oberaudorf.

Any questions you have about looking after the flat...

...can be settled later. Pack only what you need.

The laundry in the cellar and the files of invoices.

Take the insurance policies and the savings book...

...as well as the outstanding A.V. invoices...

...and the most important papers.

Felder fell at the end of March, his wife writes.

Little Drechsel stepped on a mine here yesterday...

...he's snuffed it, too. Still living are Zander...

...and maybe Kiessling. From our old group...

...there's only those two and me still here.

...P.S. Dont forget the gasmask for the boy.

RUMBLE
CLATTER

Dear Gregor, just a few quick lines before I have to go back to the field.

Everything is quiet here in the countryside. There are almost never sirens. It's like a different world.

Like the world you once spoke of.

I promise to believe in it now. We have to be even tougher, to persevere...

To endure. Then you will return...

...and then everything will be fine.

Pant
Heil Hitler.
Frau Irmina Mein-rich?
A telegram for you.
I'm sorry.

WWRRRRRRRRRR

WWRRRRRRR

RRRRRRR RRR

RRRRRRR
Hurry! Move it!

RRRR
The hay...
...has to be taken in before the rain!

RRRRRRRRR
Frieder! To the cellar!

RRRRRR
Everyone else stays here!
They're only flying to Munich anyway!

RR
To that lot with the soft hands, where they're too good to work!

That's what they get for that!
RRRRRRRH

WWRRRRRRR
RRRRRRRR
WRRRRRRRRR
RRRRRRRRR
Everyone!
The...
the Americans...
...they're
rolling through
Niederau-
dorf!

Can we go and watch them? The Americans? Please!
Later. Play a while first.
What are you doing, Mother? Are you cold?
A little, Frieder.

Let's go.

Part Three
BARBADOS

Stuttgart, 1983.
DAMEN-SALON
GRUND

Klack
Klack
Klack
Klack
ESAMTSCHULE
Klack
Klack
Klack
Klack
Klack
Klack
Klack
Klack

...and here's the headmaster's office, the nerve centre, so to speak, haha...
Oh, and this is Frau Meinrich! The backbone of the school!
Irmina, you shouldn't always work overtime.
I had work to finish.
Frau Meinrich is the school secretary. She is indispensable.
And this is Miss Crump, our new English teacher.
She's just arrived from Birmingham!
<Pleased to meet you, Mrs Meinrich.>
...
I don't think she speaks English...
Good evening, Headmaster.

Oh...

My glasses...

You're becoming forgetful, Irmina...

...yes, Frau Meinrich...

...is an institution here. She's been at the school since '47. She's got everything in hand...

...she knows ALL the thousand pupils here by name.

Really? That's incredible!

And she knows exactly who hasn't paid their dinner money.

I often see fifth years hovering around the door...

LECKER

Möbel

FRUIT
LOOM

REISPFANNE
ECO

...the Federal German Peace Movement is commemorating International Anti-War Day by blockading the US military depot
Ding dong

Elke! It's you!
I'm glad you're still awake, Irmina.

I have something for you! The postman this afternoon...
...almost didn't want to give it to me.

But I told him, there's only one Irmina here.
Even if a different surname is on the envelope.

Von Behdinger... That's my maiden name...

You were a "von"?
I didn't even know! Do tell!
It was ages ago... another time, ok? I have to be up early.

Don't forget reading club tomorrow, ok?
Of course not, Elke.
Night!

Where are my spare glasses...?

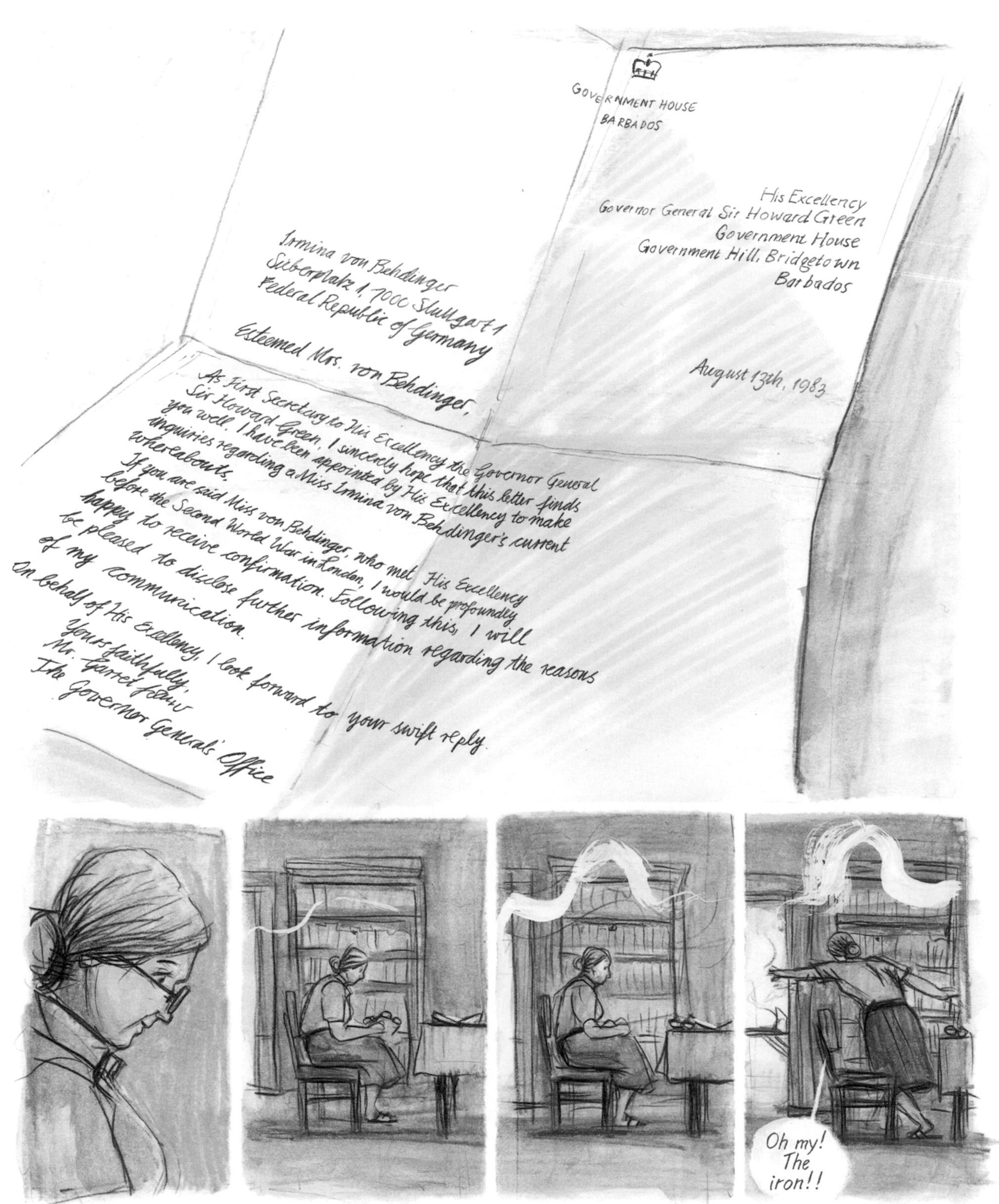

GOVERNMENT HOUSE
BARBADOS

His Excellency
Governor General Sir Howard Green
Government House
Government Hill, Bridgetown
Barbados

Irmina von Behdinger
Silberplatz 1, 7000 Stuttgart 1
Federal Republic of Germany

August 13th, 1983

Esteemed Mrs. von Behdinger,

As First Secretary to His Excellency the Governor General Sir Howard Green, I sincerely hope that this letter finds you well. I have been appointed by His Excellency to make inquiries regarding a Miss Irmina von Behdinger's current whereabouts.

If you are said Miss von Behdinger, who met His Excellency before the Second World War in London, I would be profoundly happy to receive confirmation. Following this, I will be pleased to disclose further information regarding the reasons of my communication.

On behalf of His Excellency, I look forward to your swift reply.

Yours faithfully,
Mr. Garret Fearu
The Governor General's Office

Abflu
15:35 LH 1268
15:45 SK 680
15:50 LH 278
15:55 AF 2035
16:00 LH 189
16:05 HL X3135
17:00 CO 259
17:10 LH X8630
17:30 LH 258
TOURIST
Gates
WC

parture
Condor
Cond

Dear passengers, welcome to Bridgetown, Barbados. Please remain seated with your seatbelts fastened until the plane has come to a standstill.

Thump

Jolt

Oof.

The pilot needs some practice.

Are you taking the shuttle to the Mango Bay Resort?

Excuse me?

Are you taking the **taxi** to the **hotel**?

No, I think I'm taking the bus.

COMMODORE

Oh, unlucky you. I'm being collected by the premium shuttle. The travel agency booked it as an exclusive extra for me.

I'm not going to a hotel.

Oh? Where are you staying?

With an... acquaintance on the island.

Oh boy.
Stand up straight, Irmina.

Condor
AIRPORT

Good afternoon, Madam.
Thank you...
My name is Sergeant Foster. I am here on behalf of his Excellency.
I hope you had a pleasant journey.
Thank you, Sergeant.
But... erm... where are we going?
To Government House, Madam.
His Excellency has urgent government business to attend to.
You mean... Howard?
Yes. His Excellency, Sir Howard Green, Governor General of Barbados, representative of the Crown.
Sir Howard has been actively working for the rights of the common people in the Barbados Labour Party since 1940.
Later, he founded the first University of the West Indies.
Internationally recognised, now Governor - and even knighted.
A great man, Madam.

Here we are. Your luggage will be brought to you.
You will be collected and escorted to his Excellency. Do you require anything?
N... No. Thank you, Foster.

Knock Knock
Finally...

Foster! **There** you are! I thought you had forgotten me!
I'm **Tom**, Madam. His Excellency's butler.

Please follow me, Madam.

Excellency...
...your guest is here.

Irmina!
Howard...

...

Welcome, Irmina.

My goodness, how long it has been... Thank you for making the long journey.
I have to thank **you**, Howard.

I hope you had a comfortable journey?
Oh, nothing to complain about.

It's so fast by plane...
Indeed. It is much simpler than it used to be.

Heaven forbid travelling by ship nowadays! But come, let us sit.
Let us celebrate the occasion.

Ah, Tom. What may I offer you?
Our house bar is quite well stocked.
Oh, just a glass of water, please.

Or... wait. Do you have...
...whisky?

Naturally, Madam.
But of course! A whisky. How could I have forgotten?
Will you also have one?

No, unfor-tunately not.
I no longer drink. The usual for me, Tom.
My liver, you know.

Irmina, to seeing you again.
I knew even back then that you would see the Caribbean. Do you remember?

But of course, Howard.
Tell me, how did you find me after all these years?

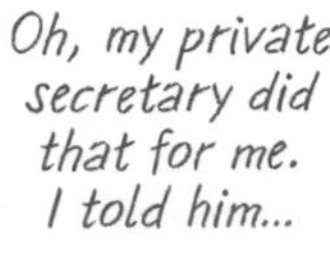
Oh, my private secretary did that for me. I told him...

...to first try in England. He also searched for the old Countess but, of course, she died long ago...
No descendants.

Oh... the Countess...

Finally, he found you in Germany. He simply searched the city registers for your first name.
Then you received his letter.

At first, I was unsure it was really you. I remembered...
...that you never wanted to return to Stuttgart of all places...

cough
Well, I certainly am happy that we found you.

Howard... I must say that I am **so** impressed! I was even greeted by your picture in the airport.
And the sergeant has told me so much. The civil rights movement, founding the university...
...and now you are governor!

Good old Foster likes to exaggerate. But it's true that I have never stopped working. Today the citizens of Barbados are thankful for what I have achieved for them and with them.
There was simply always so much to do: equal voting rights for all, independence, educational opportunities... oh...
...there was rarely pause for breath. I must say...

...I cannot really conceive of retiring in a few years.
Oh... what will you do then?
Oho, I think my Ruby has a few plans ready.

Ruby?

I will soon be able to introduce you to my wife. She is away for a few days. A charity project.

She is looking forward to meeting you when she returns.
My daughter will also be visiting then.

I'm sorry that Mr Meinrich was unable to be here.
Mr – who?
I thought...

Gregor, my husband, died almost 40 years ago.

Grenade shrapnel in the shoulder.
It was removed, but a piece travelled up his back into the brain.
It was in '44, going to the Western Front. He simply keeled over.

Oh. I didn't know that. I'm sure it was a terrible loss.
...Yes. But I still had my son. And now I have grandchildren. I've told them about you...

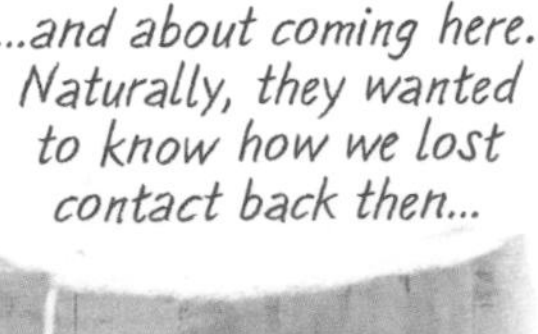
...and about coming here. Naturally, they wanted to know how we lost contact back then...

Oh yes. It was an eternity ago...
...such a turbulent time...
...and then the war...
Yes...

I must admit it is sometimes difficult to remember everything...
But that reminds me...

"Memory! A drifting board..."
"...of a ship long burst asunder – that the wind and the waves toss..."
"...abruptly from reef to reef..."

"...toward the beach!"

Klong Klong
Shakes-peare?
Almost... by an unknown contemporary of his.
Oh dear...

...nine o'clock already?
Irmina, I must excuse myself.

An important telephone call to the US awaits me.

Oh... of course. I understand. I... am also tired.

It's already the middle of the night at home...
Tom will show you to your room. We shall see each other again in the morning.

Goodnight, Howard.

Beep Beep
Madam!
Really, Madam. You cannot simply vanish without telling us where you're going.
Tom wanted to pick you up this morning and your room was empty. He was very worried.

Oh, I just wanted to see the ships.
You may be very fond of travelling, Madam, but wouldn't you like to breakfast first?

Dad, I **can't** turn up there in the small car.

Howard, my apologies. I was...
Irmina! Good morning.
May I introduce my youngest to you?

Clifford, this is Irmina Meinrich.
Good day...
You don't say... **YOU'RE** the brave Irmina?
Er...
Well, my sister will be amazed...

I have to go right now. An important appointment.
Dad, I'm taking the Ford, ok? See you this evening!
Cliff...
Bye, lady!

Sir...
Howard... your son, he looks just like you!

Like in your Oxford days...

Oh yes...
Cliff is a clever boy. But so impatient. He always has some kind of appointment.
Thank you, Tom.

Sir.
Sometimes I don't think he knows how lucky he is.
No... the young don't know how easy they have it. My son, Frieder...

...I had to be strict with him sometimes.
Does he still live near you?
Oh no! He moved 400km away with his family.
We don't see each other very often.

Forgive my asking, but have you never considered...
...remarrying?

Oh...
It never... happened. After the war...

...my goodness, there weren't any men left over!
And I wouldn't have just anybody.

Oh God, what am I blathering about?
You must have things to do.

Not right now, Irmina. Do you know what? They can live without me today. Today I'll show you the island.
We'll drive wherever you wish.

Really? Then I have a request...

Bathsheba Beach, Foster.
...to the giant rocks!

Howard! Everyone...
...waves to you!
FRUITS
It's a small island... everyone knows each other.

Look, there on the left. Chattel houses from the colonial times.
No foundations so that the workers could carry them...

The harvest hands, descendants of the slaves, had no rights for a long time.
Until the '60s, almost all the land here was planted with sugar cane.
A lot changed after independence. Now, tourists populate the beaches...
We're almost there!

Look, down there. That's where I sat.
It's exactly as you described it!
As if giants threw rocks into the water.
Can we go down there? Go swimming?
Look at the ships?
Cap'n Irmina!
Like in the past!
But...
My role demands the utmost restraint. It is a question of safety.
Of course, I understand.

That was delicious.
I wish I had a cook at home.
Haha! It wasn't always so. We used to have to scrimp and save.
When we're in our private home during the summer, Ruby cooks... or I do.

You?
That's unusual...
Of course!
When my daughter is here, we cook for Ruby together.

It sounds... like you're happy.
Oh, there are ups and downs. But Ruby has always stood by me.
And our sense of culture and art joins us.

Sir? Your evening programme is starting...
Thank you.
Irmina... perhaps you'd like to accompany me?
Yes! I'll quickly change!

Oh... no, that's not necessary. We're... staying at home.
Everything is ready, sir.

Cliff, don't tell me it's already started?

Drone

Howard...
THAT was a run!
Just look at that...
Run, boys!
...please excuse me.
Yes!

Sorry? Irmina?
I... I'm tired.
Cricket. Pah.

RRING
RRING

Howard! Good morning. Isn't it wonderful weather?
Where are we driving to today?

Oh. I see.
Of course. Your work comes first.

Good. I'll wait for Foster.
Thank you.

If I had known that you wanted to go swimming, Madam...
...I would have brought you straight here.
HOTEL
MANGO BAY
MANGO BAY

Please follow me.

The pool is here, but I have reserved a beach lounger for you.
I know you like the sea.
Please just promise me...
...that you will stay within the safety cordon.
Where can I get changed?
Safety cordon. Pah.
Like where I go each week in Leuze.
Ow!
Oh no!
Not again!
Sergeant? Excuse me...
Madam?
No, you shouldn't go into the water with cramp. But as you are at the beach, I recommend...
...for next time...
...buying different shoes.

scribble

10 December. Woke early again. The time difference is still deep in my bones. Tea with the sunrise. Now writing a travel diary.

Breakfast at eight o'clock, as always with the Governor and his son. Already a part of the family.

Got to go. Important appointment.

Invitation to dinner with Howard. Delightful hosts.

Oh yes, from Stuttgart.

Lots of talking, the context often escapes me.

That's how much I pay at home in the supermarket.
Sorry, lady. One coconut, one dollar.

12/12. Afternoon. I braved a walk to Bridgetown. Escape!

CINEMA
GLOBE
MICHAEL JACKSON'S
THRILLER
Mr Green! We've reserved the best seats for you.

14/12.
Evening. Film premiere with Howard and Clifford. We are the guests of honour. Tom and Sergeant Foster come, too.

A modern dance film. Everyone loved it. I have cramp again. Dont forget magnesium. Only 12 days left.

Official event. I stood in for his wife. I was shaking with nerves. Everyone stood up.

I wonder what impression I made?

Foster told me to "take it easy". Only 10 days left.

I ate dinner in my room. The master doesnt feel well.

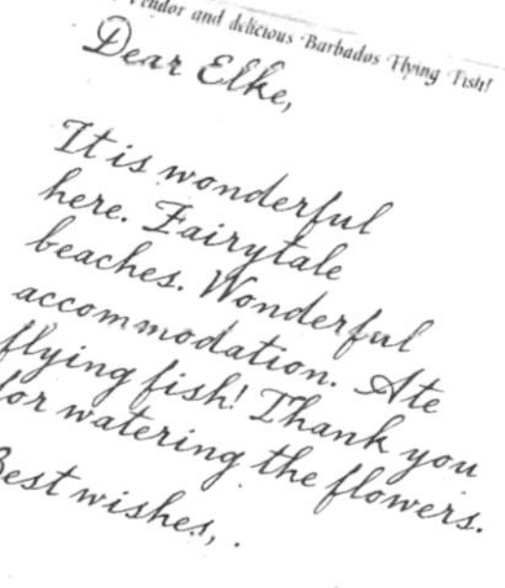

B21 Fish Vendor and delicious Barbados Flying Fish!

Dear Elke,

It is wonderful here. Fairytale beaches. Wonderful accommodation. Ate flying fish! Thank you for watering the flowers.

Best wishes,

Irmina

Elke Schrader
Sieberplatz 1
7000 Stuttgart 1
West Germany

A Best of Barbados Ltd./Nutshell Production
Photography by Dick Scoones
Printed in Barbados

16/12. Discovered a bookshop on the way to the post office! Finally, new books.

What is it you like about all those books?

BOOKS

Well, they entertain and educate. But mainly, they let me travel the world in my mind.

In your mind? And why not with your feet, lady? You've already made it to Barbados.

Haha! If you say so, Foster...

I think about my life and know very well that only two men have been important in it.

18/12. Evening together in the lounge.

At least my English is improving. Only 7 days left.

Madam, your tea.
His Excellency wishes to inform you that he is still busy.
Again?

However, he would like to remind you about the birthday reception for his daughter tomorrow evening.

Tom... are there many guests?
Oh, only around fifty, Madam.
Irmina! There you are.
May I introduce...
...our guest from Europe, Mrs Irmina Meinrich.
The Minister for Education and her husband.
My pleasure.
Really, you're called Irmina? What a coincidence...
Howard...
Er... is it?
...have you already welcomed Meyers?
Ruby! Excellent timing.

May I introduce Irmina Meinrich?
Oh...
Irmina, this is Lady Ruby...
...my wife.
Good evening.
I have been curious about you for a long time.
The brave Irmina...
Howard told me that you travelled alone to England all the way back then.
As I see, you still travel alone? And at your age? My respect.
I...
I... yes. I'm just fine on my own.
Haha, how typically European.
But please excuse me, Irmina. I must see to the guests.
See you later...
Ruby is the perfect hostess...
Now, come on, I'll introduce you to the birthday child.
Harry! Ella! How wonderful you could make it!

There she is. Follow me!
Daddy!

I would like to introduce a special guest, daughter.
Is this her, Daddy?
Excuse me, please.

This is her.
Happy Birth...
Irmina, may I introduce...

...my daughter, Irmina.
How wonderful!

What?

The surprise worked, I think.
I wanted to keep it a secret...
...until we met.

My father often told me about you.
And I finally wanted to know: who is this woman...

... who is responsible for my strange name.
Haha!

No offence meant. I've gotten used to it.

But my father promised me he'd invite you here... as a birthday present, so to speak.

Daddy, will you excuse us for a moment?

He always said that the name would help me...
...to brave my path. He told me...
Oh yes?

...that you defended him from attacks. And that you...
...wanted to become a captain! I liked that the most.
Oh, well, I had grand plans...
See, we are alike!

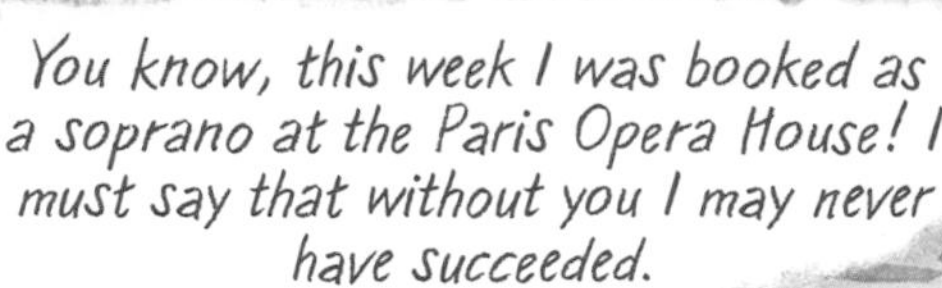
You know, this week I was booked as a soprano at the Paris Opera House! I must say that without you I may never have succeeded.

Paris! Gosh, that's not bad!
Dad wanted me to go to London.

Well, he knows I follow my own mind.
But now tell me about yourself.
I always wondered what became of your life.

My life? I... I work at a school.
Are you a teacher?
No. I... I am responsible for the organisation.
Oh, you are the headmis-tress!
Not quite, but I work closely with the headmaster.
There... there is always a mountain of work to be done.
Oh, I'm sure you're incredibly hard-working.
Your family must be very proud of you.
Hmm, if you say so...
Daddy told me how worried he was...
...when you left England. And that you lost contact.
The war and everything... it must have been terrible...
Yes... I... you know... I wanted to return to London! I had a job in Berlin at the Wa... in a Ministry...
But then...
...then my husband came along...
...and then my son.
And then the war.
And in the end...

All the destruction, all the suffering. Those terrible Nazis!

I... feel... weak...

Mrs Meinrich! Are you unwell? Oh dear...
Irmina?
I know, it's the climate.

I'll find Tom.
He'll take you to your room. You should lie down.

Irmie, it's ok. I will accompany Mrs Meinrich...
Ok, Daddy.

Howard... I... we wanted to see each other again in London.
Why... why did you leave?
Sigh
Ok.
After my exams, I applied to become a professor.
The rejection came in the return post.
Studying was acceptable. But teaching...
...that was going too far for the English...
...for someone like me. A darkie.
They even returned the application processing fee.
Very British, don't you think? Always correct.
Even in injustice.
And then...

...then
I heard about
the unrest
at home.
I took the next
ship back.

Has your
weakness
passed,
Irmina?
Oh.

My weakness...
No. No weakness
any more.
Well... then
goodnight...

Howard...

Back
then, when
my letter was
returned...
I...
I had the ticket
already. I could
have simply
sailed over...

Only...
I just wanted to
BE something.
To BE someone.
And
then...
I...

...I wasn't...
...
When your daughter...
...what could I say?
Howard, I wasn't...
...I **wasn't** brave Irmina...
Can you for—
...
...

Madam?

Would you like something to drink?

Do you have whisky?

CITY
BUS
flip
flop
flip
flop

IRMINA. LIFE IN CONTEMPORARY HISTORY. AN AFTERWORD

Dr Alexander Korb

Why are we as readers moved by the story in Barbara Yelin's comic book about the life of a young woman during the Nazi era? We tend to see immediately the alternative routes that would have allowed her to keep both her happiness and her distance from the crimes of the Nazis. In addition, we supposedly know so much about the life of Germans during this time, but in reality we simply cannot imagine what *everyday* life felt like for them. Thus the question remains: how could ordinary people, with all their dreams, problems, worries and glimpses of happiness, not only condone such a murderous system but enable it in the first place?

Obviously, the history that Barbara Yelin unrolls here has been studied in the greatest detail, and several thousand books, documentaries and movies on the topic have appeared worldwide since the 1970s. However, many contentious dialogues are still ongoing, such as the debate between Daniel Goldhagen and Christopher Browning about "ordinary Germans". This is due to the fact that the co-existence of everyday life and terror, of normality and ignominy and of life and death is a subject that always unsettles us and makes us reflect. Thinking about everyday life in the "Third Reich" raises questions on how to explain and imagine the Nazis, including their nature and their destructiveness. At the same time, Irmina's story highlights something that historians should always bear in mind: people experience the commotions of history first and foremost through their everyday lives, so that personal watersheds like first love, choosing a profession, the birth of a child or moving house can be of greater biographical significance than major historical events.

IRMINA IN THE WORLD

The historically contentious subjects that arise for discussion based on IRMINA include the Nazis' concept of "Volksgemeinschaft" (people's community) as a promise of a better society, the contradictory experiences of women under National Socialism, the terror perpetrated by the Nazis and the genocide of the Jews from the perspective of ordinary Germans. Readers are faced with the question of how a strong-willed and likeable young woman could slowly but surely become a supporter of the Nazi regime and a beneficiary of the murdering of Jews.

Irmina is an ambitious young woman who wants to make something of her life. Unlike her brothers, she wasn't able to fulfil her dream of studying at university. However, she did manage to travel to London and trained at a business school there to become a foreign language secretary. Both before and during the Nazi era, it was not unusual for young Germans, including many women, to study or work abroad. Nazi Germany was confident and saw its students as ambassadors of its new order. For example, the renowned political scientist Elisabeth Noelle-Neumann studied in the US in 1937/38 at the age of 21 with a grant from the German Academic Exchange Service.

Irmina, however, was not a student. She could neither benefit from an exchange program nor have her stay in England supported by any kind of organisation. Nevertheless, she can still be regarded as an ambassador for Germany. She is often asked about the events unfolding in Germany and unconsciously assumes a defiant attitude in defence of the regime. It certainly wasn't the case that the new regime in Germany was only ever criticised. There was also a widespread admiration of their supposed strength and ability to build. One day, Irmina comes across a demonstration of the Blackshirts, the English fascists led by Oswald Mosley, who would have been happy to cooperate with the Nazis. In his book, *Making Friends with Hitler*, the historian Sir Ian Kershaw impressively describes the background of English Nazi sympathisers.

FROM NONCONFORMIST TO NATIONAL SOCIALIST: IRMINA IN THE VOLKSGEMEINSCHAFT

Upon her return to Germany, Irmina seems to take a step closer towards her dream of independence. Her work and foreign language skills are in great demand. Prospects are good, even though her pay is low. She works hard and is not seduced by the false social promises of those in power. On the contrary, she initially maintains a cool distance from the pledges offered by the regime. However, her criticism of the system is limited to her own world and, in particular, the size of her pay cheque.

The question of how people took to the Nazis' Volksgemeinschaft, i.e. the promise of a people's community in which all "same-blooded" members would take their appropriate place, has been a central topic in Holocaust studies of the last few years. For about a decade now, historians have been debating how far Germans succumbed to the illusion that Nazism was a just form of living together, and whether Germans believed in the Nazi concept of a people's community or whether they regarded it as mere propaganda. Despite all her individualism, it is this promise that gives Irmina the feeling that the Nazi regime represents a modern system that is committed to the common good. Her husband Gregor, in particular, regularly preaches the positive and egalitarian moral values of the Nazis, such as with regard to Berlin's monumental Olympic stadium, and tries to convey to her "the spirit of the radical German reformation", while waxing lyrical about the power of a united people.

But Irmina's behaviour seems to accord with the view espoused by the late German historian Hans Mommsen, who argued that the Volksgemeinschaft was a product of propaganda which was not accepted by society at large. Irmina does not feel obliged to make any sacrifices for what is said to be the common good. On the contrary, she repeatedly asks what the Volksgemeinschaft can do for her. Yet this behaviour also leads us to the arguments put forward by those historians who have stressed that many Germans viewed National Socialism as a social promise and an opportunity to advance.

There is also the question of to what extent the regime had to use force and the threat of violence to bring the population into line. Police action and the threat of exclusion from the Volksgemeinschaft were always present. Arrests, sanctions, vilifications and concentration camps, where people were sent and released after a suitable time, were the measures used by the regime to send a message of discipline to the German population. And yet Irmina's development during the "Third Reich" shows what the historian Götz Aly called an accommodating and consensual dictatorship. After all, as decisive as the repression was, the feeling of many Germans of finally belonging to a community without necessarily being in the party was just as important. This consensus, which went beyond mere obedience, was deliberately targeted by the regime. It sought to appeal to Germans and their affections by emphasising, for example, the value of the individual "ethnic comrade" to the Volksgemeinschaft.

The racial exclusion of Jews and other groups is essential to this concept of community. The Volksgemeinschaft was not only materially based on the disappropriation of people deemed not to belong, but also manifested itself in the very idea of excluding others. Irmina completes her acceptance into the national community after her return from London when she provides "proof of ancestry from German or related blood". The fact that Irmina has no empathy for those persecuted by the regime facilitates her path into German society.

In all the steps she takes, Irmina doesn't act under duress, but develops of her own accord in a direction that stabilises the Nazi system. Irmina is certainly not suppressed. With some exceptions, she approves of the dictatorship and doesn't question the regime. She accepts all its benefits without reflection and attempts to position herself and her family to their best advantage. The fact that she doesn't play an active role in the book's scenes of people openly enriching themselves at the expense of deported or murdered Jews, such as the lootings of November 1938 or the auctioning of belongings in 1942, is probably due less to her inner distance from the events and more to her social background, upbringing and not wanting to lower herself to the level of the street. Such episodes clearly show that Nazi rule "was not a mere dictatorship from above - it was a social practice in which German society was directly involved in many ways" (Frank Bajohr). When, for example, hundreds of residents of a small town profited from the expatriation and deportation of Jews by purchasing property and belongings at low prices, took advantage of the pressures exerted on their business competitors or enjoyed promotion to jobs previously occupied by Jewish colleagues, we have clear proof that the persecution of Jews was not just a crime committed by a small clique of persecutors but that it had a wide range of effects on everyone's life, in much the same way as the behaviour of the individual had an impact on the overall course of the persecution.

WOMEN IN THE NAZI REGIME

Since the 1980s, there has been much debate on whether women should primarily be seen as victims of National Socialism or whether it actually contained a degree of emancipatory potential for non-Jewish German women. Discussions such as those between the historians Gisela Bock and Claudia Koonz soon led to a differentiated spectrum of viewpoints. On the one hand, Nazism was obviously a male-dominated and misogynistic regime with a patriarchal ideology. The Nazi seizure of power meant a clear re-masculinisation of politics, economics and society. Reactionary family policies influenced millions of women, men and children. Despite the financial support and the idealisation of the role of the mother, women were largely excluded from power and the chance to shape society.

On the other hand, the absence of men due to the war, the arms industry, the bombing campaign and the wartime society created the kind of scope for women that all wars provide. What was specific to National Socialism, however, was that the racist new order contained the potential to have an emancipating effect on non-Jewish German women. This mainly affected those women who replaced Jews at work or attained power as supervisors in concentration camps, employees in resettlement committees, assistants to the armed forces and SS or as representatives of the master race in occupied territories. The discovery of the specifically female type of perpetrator has led to research that leaves behind the traditional view of "the Nazis' women" by focusing on the special features of female perpetration and examining issues of femininity and violence. This can be found, for example, in the work of the historians Wendy Lower and Elizabeth Harvey.

Barbara Yelin uses the figure of Irmina to portray the conflict between free choice and fate. To begin with, Irmina is in full employment. Although she is low down in the pecking order at the ministry where she works and has to endure the power abuses of her superiors, her work and skills give her self-confidence and allow her to dream of promotion. Also, leaving her position and becoming a mother are decisions that Irmina and her husband make of their own free will. They both accept the supposed financial benefits of the reactionary "marriage loan" model. But Irmina can barely tolerate being reduced to the role of housewife and mother. She quickly tires of having to wait for her husband every day, doesn't want to cook for him and has no interest in the activities of the Nazi Women's League. Nevertheless, she chose her own path.

Over time, Irmina's appearance becomes noticeably haggard. Her life in the dictatorship seems to bring out her worst side. More than ever before, she focuses exclusively on her own well-being and fails to realise that she is still in a privileged position compared to the people suffering around her.

KNOWING, DECIDING, SUPPRESSING AND ASKING

As mentioned earlier, the Nazi experience of community went hand in hand with the exclusion of those deemed to be "community aliens". For this reason, the regime believed it to be of central importance to carry out the persecution of Jews in full view of the public. The comic book makes this patently clear: stores smeared with anti-Jewish slogans, looting and abuse during the November pogroms, and finally the Yellow Star from 1941. All this served to show, through means of violence, who belonged to the new society and who didn't. How did the Germans react to the exclusion, persecution and finally deportations of the Jews? Most Germans didn't want to be confronted with publicly visible violence on the streets, with chaos and wanton destruction. The November pogroms therefore caused comparatively powerful expressions of displeasure among the population, which, in turn, prompted the regime to execute most of the subsequent persecution measures away from the public eye.

Even in an anonymous city like Berlin, however, all the steps involved in the disfranchisement of Jews right up to their deportation were visible for people to see. Obviously, it's not possible to put all the reactions of the population into one bag, but it is fair to say that indifference prevailed. Irmina expresses the overriding sentiment when she says, "What have the Jews got to do with us?!". Explaining this indifference is still a matter of debate. Sir Ian Kershaw has argued that the indifference of the Germans went hand in hand with their daily concerns, while his Israeli colleague Otto Dov Kulka interprets people's readiness to turn a blind eye as silent approval. The Israeli historian David Bankier, however, sees turning a blind eye as a sign of psychological suppression. He believes that people did not want to acknowledge their participation. Quoting their alleged lack of awareness, many Germans tried to avoid being held to account later on. This also explains the widespread and loudly stated claim after the war that "we didn't know what was happening".

The question of how much the Germans knew about the genocide of the Jews is still the subject of much debate. The historian Peter Longerich recently wrote about a partial knowledge, while his colleague Bernward Dörner referred to the Holocaust as "what nobody wanted to know, but everybody could know". Stories and rumours about genocide spread all around the country among Jewish and non-Jewish Germans. There was plenty of substance to many of these stories, which is no surprise since hundreds of thousands of Germans in occupied territories in the East came into direct or indirect contact with mass murder. Whereas the mass shooting of Jews in the occupied parts of the Soviet Union was somewhat better known, the picture changes when it comes to the genocide in extermination camps like Auschwitz. In this case, concrete details were as good as unknown because the SS succeeded in sealing off the mass murders from the general public. Rumours about gassing were the exception. Although historians still argue about what exactly the Germans might have known, they agree on one point: the German population could have known a lot about the genocide if it had wanted to. After all, fragments of information were available for people to put together and common sense could have made them draw the conclusion that the Jews deported to the East would probably not survive.

This also clarifies the fact that knowledge, just like suppression of knowledge, is a process that individuals shape actively. Whenever Irmina is confronted with violence towards Jews, either as an eye-witness or when hearing rumours, she refuses to accept the reality. Originally, she wasn't an anti-Semite and went shopping at a "Jewish" department store up to 1938. However, she comes to back the increasingly violent Nazi policies towards Jews by forbidding others to speak their minds: "Not another word, Gerda. I don't want to hear any more. I really should report you." She and her husband help each other during moments of weakness and moral doubt, thereby creating a way to turn a blind eye together. The Nazis strengthened such a "community of guilt" by reinforcing the propaganda against the Jews in the second half of the war. Irmina's behaviour shows how the Holocaust didn't produce feelings of sympathy among Germans but, on the contrary, strengthened their anti-Semitic resentments. Irmina seems to sense the inner damage being done inside her, but makes the Jews responsible for it. "The Jews are our misfortune!" she exclaims to her son.

ALTERNATIVE PATHS

The reader already suspects that Irmina's thoughts about a life she never led are not just a form of projection. Irmina wrestles with herself, the path she took in life, the decisions she made and the love she never lived. Could her love for Howard also have led her to reject the Nazis' racism? What would have happened if she'd not only emigrated to England but also followed him to Barbados? It's impossible to say what might have become of these alternative possibilities. From an historical perspective, however, it is important to point out that these possibilities would have existed.

The character of Howard is far from just a projection screen for Irmina, as he seeks and finally goes his own path. As German as Irmina's own story might appear, her stage is actually the globality of the 20th century, which is not least based on Europe's colonialism and imperialism. In this sense, Barbara Yelin touches upon a current trend in research that focuses on the lives of black people in Europe. Irmina's biography also shows how Germany was embedded in a Europe that was never as white as the Nazis imagined it to be.

Irmina had a full range of possibilities. Yet the fact that she chose the Nazi path from the wide variety in front of her, encompassing feminism, internationality and individuality, makes her story typical of this time. It was just as typical that she failed to find happiness in fascism, like millions of others.

Irmina thinks about her past and reflects on the decisions she made. However, this doesn't go so far as to include her support of the Nazi regime. She doesn't seem to question her own role as a wife of an SS man, as a silent eyewitness and, at least indirectly, as a beneficiary of the persecution of Jews. German responsibility for the Second World War and the genocide of the Jews does not seem to form part of her thoughts.

There is, moreover, an empty space due to the fact that she refused to allow events to get close to her as an eye- and ear-witness, choosing instead to occupy herself with more mundane activities. Irmina belongs to a generation mainly known for its silence. This doesn't seem to be a silence of something that one could talk about if one chose to. Rather, the active process of suppression, which took hold immediately during the events to be suppressed, led to a speechlessness that could barely be overcome. The Nazi propaganda of portraying the Jews as the aggressors, blaming them for their own persecution and presenting the German people as war victims only strengthened this process. After being confronted by their children or grandchildren, not many people from this generation were willing to open up and try to answer questions. In any case, the questions were not asked often enough.

After the passing of this rather speechless generation, we are left only with attempts to create a reconstruction from the empty spaces of memory. Barbara Yelin's graphic novel shows how enlightening it is to set out on such a pursuit.

Dr Alexander Korb *is Senior Lecturer at the University of Leicester and Director of the Stanley Burton Centre for Holocaust and Genocide Studies. In various books and articles, Korb has researched Nazi violence, people's reactions to it and the question of similarities and differences between the Holocaust and other cases of genocide in the 20th century.*

THANK YOU:

My editor Christian Maiwald for the excellent dramaturgical and comic book-specific project support from conception to final panel.

Dr Alexander Korb for the knowledgeable advice and afterword. Thank you also to Sarah Ehlers and Professor Stefan Link.

For their many ideas and sharp eyes for images, text and dramaturgy: Johanna Richter, Christina Ackermann, Nina Pagalies, Tilmann Pusch, Maria Luisa Witte, Jutta Pilgram, Susann Reck, Reinhard Kleist; particularly Ludmilla Bartscht for her readiness to help to the very end; Luise Schricker and Moritz Friedrich for the energetic support with scanning and retouching.

Ineka Beige and Padma for the endless advice, knowledge and friendship.

My family for its support and trust.

Martin Friedrich for the thousands of tips, for enduring readiness to talk and for the colours in this book (and in everything else).

Barbara Yelin, was born in 1977 in Munich and studied illustration at the Hamburg University of Applied Sciences. She became known as a comic book artist in France for LE VISITEUR and LE RETARD. Her first publication in Germany was GIFT, based on a script by Peer Meter. This story of a historical criminal case brought her to the attention of a larger audience in Germany. She has subsequently published a collection of her RIEKES NOTIZEN comic strips, which were originally printed in Germany in the daily newspaper Frankfurter Rundschau.

Barbara Yelin was a co-publisher of the anthology SPRING for many years and gives workshops around the world. She lives and works in Munich.